Boaters and Broomsticks

Tales & Historical Lore of the Erie Canal

By the same author:

LOW BRIDGE! FOLKLORE AND THE ERIE CANAL
WALTER D. EDMONDS, STORYTELLER

7 Dock Street, circa 1860, unknown artist.

Boaters
and Broomsticks

Tales & Historical Lore
of the Erie Canal

LIONEL D. WYLD

North Country Books, Inc.
Utica, New York

Boaters and Broomsticks
Tales & Historical Lore of the Erie Canal

by

Lionel D. Wyld

Library of Congress Cataloging-in-Publication Data
Wyld, Lionel D.
  Boaters and Broomsticks.

  1. Erie Canal (N.Y.)—History. 2. Erie Canal Region
(N.Y.)—History. 3. Erie Canal Region (N.Y.)—Social life
and customs. 4. Folklore—New York (State)—Erie Canal
Region. I. Title.
F127.E5W89 1987 974.7'96 86-28556
ISBN 0-932052-45-2 (pbk.)

North Country Books, Inc.
Utica, New York 13051

For Jamie, Jason, J. Michael, and Tyler

Versions of several tales and folk stories collected by the author appeared previously in various articles and were included or mentioned in his *Low Bridge! Folklore and the Erie Canal* (Syracuse University Press). Sketches of the canal engineers are adapted from those the author prepared for *40' x 28' x 4': The Erie Canal—150 Years* (Oneida County Erie Canal Sesquicentennial Commemoration Commission), for which he was Editor.

Contents

Preface

Folklore is many things. It is many things in upstate New York. It is the Union College ghost and the Legend of the Baker's Dozen. The tales of the Thunder God Hinum at Niagara and the exploits of Indian fighter Tom Quick. The Revolutionary scout Tim Murphy who would bend his rifle barrel on his knee crescent-like in order to shoot deer running around boulders. The folk pageant of the Mormons at Palmyra and the adventures of Catskill's John Darling. The Cardiff Giant at Cooperstown and the oversize fish in the Erie Canal. It is wishing on a new load of hay and starting public projects by being sure the left foot goes on the shovel first for good luck at a groundbreaking. Professor C.L. Wallis, former editor of *New York Folklore Quarterly* and author of numerous books, called folklore "an investigation of the ways ordinary people did things." Maybe that's as good a definition as any other.

Canal boaters of the nineteenth century have provided us with some of our most culturally significant lore, although, to be sure, in this age of supersonic transportation, it often seems anachronistic to think of canal boats as wondrous carriers of goods and people gliding along at the miraculous rate of four miles an hour. Yet, that was the case, and it all started with the completion in

1825 of "Clinton's Ditch" (or whatever other term one chooses to denote the historic and famous inland waterway across New York State); whether the name we give it is "Big Ditch," "Grand Western Canal," or "Old Erie," any of them seems today to suggest a romantic and nostalgic era. The Erie ushered in, without question, America's "Canal Era." Its boaters were big and bragging, for the Erie Canal was, after all, the longest and the best inland waterway ever built. A miraculous achievement, the people called it; and no one could or can dispute the triumph of engineering, pioneering know-how, and plain Yorker perseverance and fortitude that the building of the Erie represented. Towpath soil and Erie water proved a fertile medium for the nurture of a folklore; and the self-conscious urge of the people, the folk, to perpetuate the bigness and the bragging — in short, to legendize it — was impossible to prevent. The giant squash, the oversize fish (one pulled a canal boat all the way from Lockport, New York, to Detroit, Michigan!), the whopper frogs and polliwogs, the towrope-walking mules, the locktender-boater-log rafter feuds, the boaters' superstitions (put a new broom on the bow of the canal boat to ward off witches) — all of these and more provide an accumulated cultural inheritance that is part fact, part fancy, part tradition, and — sometimes — part literary invention.

The canal itself stretched some 363 miles from Buffalo and Lake Erie to Albany in the East, and there were eighty-three locks, including twenty-seven between Albany and Schenectady alone (a 15-mile distance as the crow flies). It's true that it was only a "damp ditch" by today's standards — after all, its prism or trough was but forty feet across at the surface and the depth of the canal was only four feet. But still this project which began in 1817 was a stupendous achievement for a young country. Across the Atlantic, England had a hundred canals at this time, but no single British canal was very long. Russia had a 4500-mile inland water route, although no part of it was more than half the length of New York's Erie. France's impressive Languedoc Canal, an already famous European waterway, ran a little over a hundred miles. As upstate New York author Samuel Hopkins Adams wrote in *Grandfather Stories*, his wonderful collection of reminiscences about the Erie Canal's early days, "the Grand Western Canal was the pride and glory of the nation, vaunted as the eighth wonder of the world." When the Erie Canal was completed, Pennsylvania and other states in the East and the Midwest began canal projects, and Canada's Royal Engineers began constructing their beautiful and still operating Rideau Canal system. But the Old Erie seems to have retained its historic aura and remains the most colorful of all.

The Erie Canal is, rightly enough, one of New York State's most cherished and fascinating topics, yet it provides only a small piece of the plethora of folklore material that is potentially available in the Empire State. For folklore embraces legends, tales, ghost stories, ballads and songs, proverbs, and the rustic ways of doing things: almost anything of an unsophisticated nature orally transmitted from mother to daughter, father to son, generation to generation — often followed even when not believed, practiced and held to be true by some, passed on as habit by others. Folklorists and historians often work hand in hand to uncover the rich mines of material in upstate New York, just as in many another region of the United States. The charms, superstitions, beliefs, cures, and signs that were once a firm part of the culture frequently are found to continue to have an accepted place in the behavior and customs of the present day.

History and folklore are not static, and rarely is the "digging" dull. Looking into the traditions of the past, collecting the ballads and tall tales of folklore or the more tangible artifacts that go into historical societies and museum displays are fascinating and culturally important endeavors. Important, too, is developing an interest of the youth of one's state or locality in their heritage, letting a new generation sense something of the ways their ancestors did things, how they sang, what they laughed and cried about, how they bragged or fought or romanced, and what they did to earn a livelihood.

Here are some stories and tales of the Erie boaters and of the days when "canawling" was in flower. I hope you like them.

Acknowledgment

I am especially grateful to the many persons who provided stories and tales, bits of song material, photographs, and old newspaper clippings that have provided rich ore for historical mining. In omitting the very many individual names of correspondents and other informants who shared their stories, some of them highly personal, with me, the exclusion in no way reflects a lack of appreciation. Similarly, whenever liberty has been taken in changing the wording for the purposes of narrative style or in organizing the material, it in no way mitigates that appreciation.

Boaters and Broomsticks

Tales & Historical Lore of the Erie Canal

The Erie Canal in the early 1830's.

Chapter 1

What's In a Name?

The Erie Canal has had a number of aliases in its long history. At first, it was known as "Clinton's Ditch," in deference to the great Governor DeWitt Clinton who worked so hard to make the dream of an inland waterway a reality in upstate New York. But to some groups, political opponents and those unsure of the outcome or the need to spend so much time and money in those days, it was equally regarded as "Clinton's Folly."

Gradually, as the project begun in 1817 neared completion, the farsightedness of Governor Clinton and the canal proponents became more and more acknowledged. The term "Big Ditch" became one of awe more than of contempt. "Big Ditch" was short, but appropriate — although *big* suggested the magnitude of the project and length rather than otherwise, when one considers the canal was just four feet deep. Some early nineteenth century folk, New Yorkers who were proud of the State's accomplishment, liked to refer to the waterway as "The Grand Western Canal"; and that's the way it appeared in many tourist guidebooks and gazetteers of the times. Sometimes, it was simply called "The Grand Canal." As the years passed and the Erie was enlarged once, twice, and then again to become part of the New York State Barge Canal system, the term "Old Erie" came into use for referring to the original canal that first linked Buffalo and Lake Erie to Albany and the eastern ports.

Along the way, of course, boaters had their own terms for the canal. To many who worked the mule-powered or horse-drawn packets and freight boats, the Erie was "The Roaring Giddap." Just as the packet boats took their name from the sleek boats of the Atlantic run, so the boaters on them had a nautical stance worthy of the best seamen; thus, it was only natural for the Erie to be called, at times, "The Horse Ocean." And, thanks perhaps to the inventiveness of some unknown balladeer, whose talent became coupled with that curious American pride and brag that marks the country's folk heroes, the canal became "The Raging Erie" of song (with the name often drawled out into a longish "Ee-rye-ee"), a formidable seaway that could test the brawniest of men with its seething and stormy waters!

"Old Erie" is a nostalgic phrase now. It has that good-old-days ring to it, when travel on a canal packet was the height of luxury, transportation at four-miles-an-hour was a pretty fast clip, and the nation was young in spirit.

Chapter 2

Whose Idea
Was It, Anyway?

While no one can doubt the historic reality of the Erie Canal, the history leading up to that magnificant accomplishment is not always clear. Certainly, one of the more interesting questions for historians and other writers about the canal is that of the originator of an *"Erie* Canal."

Credit generally is given to Gouverneur Morris, although another ardent proponent, Jesse Hawley, also has a valid claim. Like the authorship of the plays that bear Shakespeare's name, the question of originator is largely an academic one, but in actuality at least these two claimants may both be right.

As early as 1800, Gouverneur Morris remarked in a letter written in December of that year that ships from London might be made to sail through Hudson's River into Lake Erie; and in 1803, in writing the Surveyor-General of New York, Simeon DeWitt, Morris spoke of creating an artificial river from Lake Erie to the Hudson. History thus records that Gouverneur Morris was the first person to document the idea of a continuous upstate New York canal (his "artificial river").

Jesse Hawley made a long and determined effort to influence the judgment of history in his direction. His claim to being first involves a series of articles signed "Hercules" which appeared in the *Genesee Messenger* during 1807 and 1808. In these articles, Hawley/Hercules concentrated public opinion on an Erie Canal project. He was not the originator of the idea, but he wanted to be credited, he said, with "the original and first publication of a project for the overland route of the Erie Canal, from Buffalo to

Jesse Hawley

the Hudson." In this he was correct, and the "Hercules" articles actually went a long way in focusing public opinion on a trans-state canal. More than any other person, including Governor DeWitt Clinton himself, who backed the idea and promoted it to successful completion, the less generally known figure, Jesse Hawley, may well deserve more recognition than history seems to have accorded him.

Who thought up the idea of a canal in the first place? James Geddes, later to be named one of the principal Erie engineers, said that canal linkages "must have been contemplated by the first navigators on these waters," and his assumption is doubtless a valid one.

As early as 1724, a hundred years before the Erie, the New York colonial governor's surveyor-general, Cadwallader Colden, prepared a report on the "Furr-Trade" that led to a survey for a trade route from Albany to Lake Ontario, but it wasn't until the

22

1780's that anything resembling progress was made toward realizing significant or lasting changes. Even then, the continuous canal idea was pretty far from becoming a reality. General George Washington saw the area as the "seat of empire" when he visited Fort Stanwix (Rome) in 1784, and the General mentioned the possibility for an east-west water route across what became, prophetically — or perhaps because of his phrasing — the Empire State. Within a few years an Irish immigrant engineer named Christopher Colles submitted a plan to the New York Legislature for removing obstructions to navigation on the Mohawk river, and Colles's proposals stressed the advantages of inland navigation between Albany and the Oswego region. In the State legislature, Long Island assemblyman Jeffrey Smith introduced an act to improve navigation along the Mohawk route. It called for "extending the same, if practicable, to Lake Erie." This was probably the first recorded instance of the term "Erie" in connection with an inland water navigation proposal.

In 1791, banker and agriculturist Elkanah Watson, an early proponent of public support for turnpikes and canals, toured western New York, kept a journal of his trip, and influenced General Philip Schuyler to similar pursuits. His Western Inland Navigation Company received a charter to improve the water route from the Hudson River to Seneca Lake and Lake Ontario, and some work was accomplished. In February 1808, Joshua Forman introduced a resolution in the Assembly for a canal to join the Hudson River with Lake Erie, and in 1810, following a similar resolution in the Senate, seven canal commissioners were appointed to study the feasibility of a canal across the state.

The result was the Grand Western Canal. The next step would be the start of construction at Rome, New York, in 1817. It would reconfirm both a patriotic tradition and one of folklore — begin public projects on the Fourth of July and be sure the left foot goes on the spade when turning the initial shovelful at a groundbreaking.

HISTORIC NEW YORK
THE ERIE CANAL - JULY 4, 1817

The ceremonies outside the village of Rome on Independence Day, 1817, climaxed years of discussion about building the Erie Canal. Dignitaries and local citizens assembled at sunrise to attend the start of construction. Judge Joshua Hathaway, a veteran of two American wars, spoke and began the excavation. Judge John Richardson, the first contractor, then turned the earth. Cannon boomed as others started digging.

Benjamin Wright, "the father of American engineering," assisted by John B. Jervis, supervised construction of the section between Utica and the Seneca River. In the first year, 15 miles were constructed. By October, 1819, the 98-mile section was complete, and the first boat traveled from Rome to Utica.

When finished in 1825, the Erie Canal was considered the foremost engineering achievement of the time. The 363-mile Canal crossed the State and became the main route between the Atlantic Ocean and the Great Lakes. Western New York flourished with new, cheap transportation. The canal insured the place of New York City as the nation's greatest port and city, and it hastened development of the Mid-West.

The modernized State Barge Canal System, consisting of the Erie, Champlain, Oswego and Cayuga-Seneca Canals, was completed in 1918.

NEW YORK STATE EDUCATION DEPARTMENT 1967

Historical marker set up at Rome, New York for the 1967 Erie Canal sesquicentennial, commemorating the beginning of canal construction.

Photo by D. Tranquille, Utica

Chapter 3

Canals, Canals

The Grand Erie Canal was hailed far and wide as the longest canal in the world, and it was, without doubt, of great historical influence. In opened the West, brought prosperity to New York State, and established New York City as a prominent shipping port. But the canal that opened in 1825 was not the first in the United States.

An earlier canal was built during the American Revolution between Mechanicville and Stillwater in northeastern New York State, to provide a means of transportation around the river rapids; and early canal links, on the route of the later Erie Canal, were built around the Mohawk River village of Little Falls, New York, and in the Wood Creek area near Rome, where an Indian portage had long connected with the Mohawk. The Western Inland Lock Navigation Company's Rome Canal was dug in 1797 to eliminate this portage. It provided an artificial waterway with a lock at each end of the canal. From the early 1700's batteaus from Schenectady were poled up the Mohawk River to the Upper Landing at Rome, if water depth permitted. In dry seasons, they stopped at what was known as the Lower Landing. Goods were carried overland to Wood Creek at Brodock's Corners. Improvement on the Creek began in the mid-1700's. During the six years after the Rome Canal was dug, other dams and locks were built to improve the navigation between the old Upper and Lower Landings of Wood Creek.

To avoid lockage at Rome and maintain the long level from Frankfort to Syracuse, the Erie Canal of 1817 at Rome was dug through the swamp about a quarter of a mile south of the earlier Rome Canal. Interestingly enough, the enlarged Erie Canal, which opened to traffic in this area in 1844, returned to a more northerly route, while the present Barge Canal, completed in 1918, again passed south of Rome.

After the Erie Canal opened in 1825, canals literally sprang up all over the Eastern seaboard and inland into today's Midwest — from Pennsylvania, Delaware, Maryland, and Virginia to Ohio and Indiana. One of the most ambitious ideas which was put forth in those days of early "canal fever" came from residents of Troy, New York, who in 1825 voted to build a canal that would run from Troy to Boston, Massachusetts, right over the rugged Berkshire Mountains. It was not one of the canal ideas that caught on.

A Massachusetts canal, however, the Middlesex Canal, did provide an early and important transportation link for Boston merchants. In June, 1793, the Governor of Massachusetts, John Hancock, signed a document incorporating "James Sullivan, Esquire & others" as proprietors of the Middlesex Canal "for the purpose of cutting a Canal from the waters of Merrimack River into the waters of Medford River." The canal was twenty-seven and a quarter miles long, with twenty locks and eight aqueducts. Albert Gallatin called it in 1808 "the greatest work of the kind which has been completed in the United States." As a result of that canal, continuous water passage was possible to Boston, the state capital, and Concord, New Hampshire. Part of the old

Middlesex Canal was restored in the Billerica area, between Boston and Lowell, by the Middlesex Canal Association in the 1970's.

The Delaware Canal, along with the Lehigh Canal and other divisions of an extensive canal system across Pennsylvania, contributed importantly to that state's economy, and today the restoration and maintenance of the Delaware Canal, now incorporated into the Theodore Roosevelt State Park running south from Easton and designated a National Historic Landmark, provides a 59-mile towpath trail along its length open to the public.

Across the Delaware River at Lambertville and Washington's Crossing, the state of New Jersey has similarly renovated and restored the Delaware and Raritan Canal. As a matter of fact, the entire canal, which opened in 1834 to connect Philadelphia with New Brunswick and New York City, has become a kind of outdoor public museum of American transportation history. It, too, is on the Registry of Historic Places. Similar stories could be written about other canals, like the Chesapeake and Ohio Canal in the East, and the Wabash and Erie Canal in Indiana.

And also about the Erie. There are canal parks at Black Rock, Lock Berlin, Wide Waters (Auburn), Palmyra Aqueduct, Macedon, and one with a National Landmark just north of Camillus, where the Nine Mile Creek Aqueduct arched the Erie. In central upstate New York a section of the famed Erie Canal from Rome to Fayetteville, a village east of Syracuse named for the Marquis de Lafayette, has been cleared and redeveloped by preservationists. At Rome itself, where the first shovel of earth was turned to start the canal construction in 1817, visitors to Erie Canal Village can even take a ride on a horse-drawn replica of a nineteenth century Erie canal boat.

Members and guests of the Canal Society of New York State enjoy a ride on the replica nineteenth century canal boat at Erie Canal Village at Rome.

Photo by Damon Williams, Jr., Boston

Chapter 4

How the Grand Erie Canal Saved Christmas

Everyone has heard Dr. Seuss's story of "How the Grinch Stole Christmas," but there was a time New Netherland, as the eastern part of New York State was once known, almost lost it. Here's how it happened.

St. Nicholas was visiting old Albany, or Fort Orange, which was part of New Netherland, in preparation for his annual distribution of New Year cookies during the Christmas season. He was exceedingly kindhearted and generous, of course, and probably responsible, for all we know, for the good Dutch devising the "Baker's Dozen" idea which, legend has it, began in Fort Orange. Anyway, during his visit that particular year of 1825, St. Nick was troubled as he gradually came to realize that the people of New Netherland were becoming an incorrigible lot, with the burghers growing rich on useless and eccentric urban "improvements" that didn't really improve anything or help anyone. As further evidence to this backsliding, they committed the sacrilege of pulling down the ancient and honourable Dutch church, which stood right in the middle of State Street, or Staats-Street as it was called then.

At this, the good St. Nicholas was sorely upset. In his bitterness he resolved to return to his homeland and leave the city to be swallowed up in its own degradation. In a melancholy mood, then, he betook himself through the streets, to make his last farewell, when he came to the outlet of the Grand Canal, just then completed.

"Is het mogelyk?" he exclaimed — "Is it possible?" — for he was delighted to see this proof that his beloved people had not altogether degenerated from their industrious and creative ancestors. He decided he better not leave them to strange saints, after all.

He took a ride on the new Erie Canal and returned in such measureless content, it is said, that he blessed the good city of Fort Orange. He even resolved to distribute a more than usual store of his New Year cookies at the Christmas holydays.

"Entrance of the Erie Canal into the Hudson" by James Eights, 1823.

Chapter 5

The Lockport Combines

In 1825, a visitor to Lockport, New York, would have witnessed a marvel of engineering in the young United States of America. At a time when there wasn't a single native-born engineer in the country, a flight of canal locks had been designed and built that were, said the journalists and foreign tourists, the rival of the Old World's pyramids or the Collossus at Rhodes.

When Esek Brown opened a tavern in 1820, Lockport was only a clearing in the forest at the edge of the Niagara escarpment. His neighbors were less than a hundred all told. By the end of 1821, their number had grown to over two thousand, as carpenters, masons, blacksmiths, teamsters, and merchants were drawn to the area by the building of the "twin fives." Irish canal workers built their own "Irish town," and the village kept growing amid the bustle of construction and smoke of blasting powder, one of the first towns in the new nation to come about because of a major public project. By 1822 it became the Niagara County seat, with its own post office and newspaper, the *Lockport Observer*.

Lockport is about half way between Rochester and Buffalo, which was the Erie Canal's western terminus. At Lockport five pairs of locks ("combines" they were called) lifted the Erie Canal

31

over the Niagara Escarpment, a geological phenomenon left over from the glacial age; and before the canal had been in operation very long every tourist and traveller was talking about the famous "Lockport Five." Where most Erie locks were single locks that only permitted passage in one direction at a time, these were a series of five double locks that allowed eastbound and westbound boats to go through lockage at the same time.

Equally impressive, at the western end of the village, was the "Deep Cut," where nearly two miles of canal trough had to be cut through the solid rock. This excavation alone required removal of 1,477,700 cubic yards of material!

It is little wonder that Lockport on the Erie Canal proved to be such a thrilling place for nineteenth century tourists. Its five combines were among the miraculous technical accomplishments that made the Grand Western Canal a marvel of engineering in its day.

"Lockport on the Erie Canal" by Mary Keys, 1832.

Munson-Williams-Proctor Institute, Utica

Chapter 6

The Erie on China

The War of Independence was scarcely over when British potters began to export their china to the new American states. All sorts of patriotic designs, leading political figures and heroes, and scenic views were used as decoration to entice buyers in the young nation. These designs were printed on plates, pitchers and other dishes, and shops everywhere stocked them.

English potters decorated their earthenware by an inexpensive method known as transfer-printing. It involved no handwork because the design was engraved on a copper plate and could be reproduced over and over. Although neither the finest nor the most expensive of china, shopkeepers and peddlers in the United States had little trouble selling the English product. Much of it was manufactured in the Staffordshire district of England, and some in Liverpool. Transfer-printed pottery became synonymous with Staffordshire, and the china wares have become known popularly as "Staffordshire" or "Old Blue."

It wasn't always blue, however. Black was the first color used for this transfer-printing process; it was a color favored by Liverpool manufacturers whose wares flourished in the period from 1770 to 1830. Staffordshire potters became known for blue and carmine ware in the eighteenth and early nineteenth centuries, with the brilliant, rich-hued plates and other pieces, being the most popular. Over a dozen potters specialized in it, including James & Ralph Clews, John & William Ridgeway, J. & J. Jackson, Ralph Stevenson, and Joseph Stubbs. By the War of 1812, the United States had been inundated with Staffordshire, and by the time of Lafayette's visit in 1824, England manufactories were in high gear. Almost every step of the general's tour was covered in blue Staffordshire.

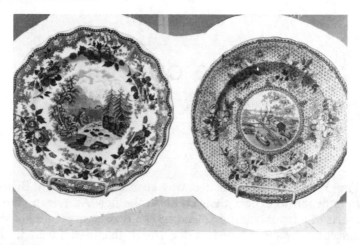

Staffordshire china of the 1820's commemorating the Erie Canal (left, Little Falls plate; right, Buffalo plate) in the collection of the Buffalo and Erie County Historical Society.

Photo by D. Tranquille, Utica

So, too, was the Erie Canal. Part of a series by Ralph Stevenson featured a scene depicting the opening of the canal in 1825, along with cameo-size portraits of Jefferson, Washington, Lafayette, and DeWitt Clinton — rather an eclectic foursome since Jefferson never believed a canal was possible and had turned down a request for national sponsorship, and the Marquis de Lafayette, while a national hero because of his part in the American Revolution, was a French citizen who had nothing to do with Erie history except that he rode on a canal boat on the Erie Canal during his visit as guest of the nation.

Chapter 7

A French General on the Erie Canal

Among the many distinguished travellers who rode Erie water, perhaps none was more well known or better liked than the Marquis de Lafayette, one of the heroes of the American struggle for independence. When he came to the United States at his own expense, he had been made a major general by Congress. His visit to the United States in 1824 and 1825 was unique, for never before had a government sent such an invitation to a private citizen of a foreign country. He was Guest of the Nation, invited by a resolution of Congess and President James Monroe. Legislative acts of Virginia and Maryland had made him forever a citizen of those states and of America. He came in August 1824 with his son, George Washington Lafayette; his secretary, Lavasseur; and his valet, Bastien. Monsieur Marie Joseph Paul Yves Roch Gilbert du Motier was back in America.

Here he was the Marquis again, France having long since abolished the title, and he was among friends. In New York, speeches, banquets, and receptions seemed endless, and throngs of people met him wherever he went. Samuel F.B. Morse, long before he invented the telegraph, painted his portrait for the city, and the artist Sully did one for Independence Hall in Philadelphia. In Boston, he met former President John Adams, then

Lafayette, engraving from a print by Leroux,
after a painting by Scheffer published in Paris in
1824.

89 years old, and in New Hampshire he slept in a bed his beloved comrade General George Washington had slept in. His travels brought him into contact with contemporary American literary figures, and some later to become famous. The young Ralph Waldo Emerson, for example, and a teenage Oliver Wendell Holmes saw him as he made his way through Cambridge, Lexington, and Concord; and a year later he greeted a 6-year-old boy named Walt Whitman in Brooklyn.

In March, 1825, Lafayette began his great journey, one that was to take him through the American South and West, then north to Buffalo and over the Erie Canal to Albany and, by horse and stagecoach, on to Boston again for the fiftieth anniversary of the Battle of Bunker Hill on June 17, 1825.

At Buffalo, old Red Jacket, Chief of the Senecas, greeted him. As he journeyed eastward on the Erie and passed under a canal bridge, a young Indian jumped down on the deck of his boat and cried out, "Where is Kayewla?" This was the name the Oneidas had given him in 1778, and, hearing it, Lafayette said, "I am Kayewla."

"I am the son of Onekachekoeta," said the Indian youth, to let the French visitor know he was the son of the Oneida chief who had returned to France with the Marquis after the war.

The Frenchman's tour on the Erie Canal took him through Oneida Country in June, 1825, several months before the official opening that marked the completion of the canal in October of that year. The canal had been virtually completed, however, and allowed navigation for most of its distance. When Lafayette's group of boats came down from Buffalo, the Erie Canal was lighted by a hundred torches as the General's boat arrived at Rome about 10 o'clock the night of June 9. A committee from Rome, Utica, and Whitesboro extended greetings, and a group of Rome ladies with bouquets honored the distinguished visitor. Colonels B. P. Johnson, Ardon Seymour, and E. A. Foster represented Rome's military organizations.

The General's packet, appropriately named the *Governor Clinton* specially for the occasion, stopped at Rome, where the company disembarked, followed by members of his party in other boats making up the entourage. They proceeded to the American Hotel, located at the corner of James and Dominick Streets, where Lafayette was officially welcomed by Wheeler

Barnes, a prominent Rome lawyer.

Following an hour-long reception and much handshaking, the General and his party boarded their boats and proceeded to Oriskany, where Lafayette stayed the night with Colonel Gerrit Lansing, who had been under his command at the surrender of Cornwallis, commander of the British forces at Yorktown in October 1781. The next morning the visitors went to Whitesboro — called Whitehall Landing on some early maps — where the Marquis was seated in an armchair on a raised platform in front of the residence of Jonas Platt. He wanted to know if the good woman was still living who made such a nice johnny-cake. Lafayette had been in the area in 1784 on his way to attend the treaty signing that year at Fort Stanwix. On being informed that the woman still lived — she was the widow of Hugh White — he again called upon her and was treated to a freshly baked cake.

The village had organized a parade for the occasion. The procession with General Lafayette seated in a barouche along with Whitesboro's Judge Williams, was preceded by an escort of cavalry led by General John J. Knox. All along the route the houses and fences were lined with people eager to pay their respects to the guest of the nation. At the village line, the procession was given a 24-gun salute in General Lafayette's honor.

The procession then turned into Lafayette Square, which was the former "Canal Street" newly renamed. A triumphal arch, mounted on a bridge over the canal, was inscribed "Lafayette, the Apostle of Liberty, we hail thee — Welcome," and from there the group moved down Genesee Street to Shepherd's Hotel, where Lafayette was received on the steps by William Clarke, who was president of the village of Utica. (The term "mayor" was not used until later in the nineteenth century.) Following speeches by Clarke and the Marquis, numerous men and ladies of Oneida County were introduced to the visitor, at whose special request the chiefs of the Oneida Indians were also invited to meet with him. Two of these he recognized from the Revolutionary War campaign.

His party reboarded their canal boats, and the Marquis de Lafayette went back to the *Governor Clinton*, which had been outfitted in elegant style for the occasion. It was drawn by three white horses, also in splendid trappings, and with mounted horsemen in uniform. As the boat left for the eastward journey,

38

another 24-gun salute was fired, and the area's townspeople jammed the bridges and canal banks, cheering loudly and continuously until the Marquis' entourage had passed on its way to Schenectady.

Chapter 8

Old Dorp

Old Dorp — or Schenectady, if you prefer the regular name for what one canaller is alleged to have called "the Dutchest damned town in the state" — grew with the Erie Canal; but there seemed to be little optimism in 1825 in that upstate New York town on the banks of the Mohawk River. Schenectady's citizens, along with those in Rome, New York, where the canal construction had begun in 1817, refused to enter into the gala celebration which climaxed the building of the Erie Canal and its official opening in October 1825. They surmised that the canal would really mean a loss of business for them. Perhaps they thought only of a possible increased trade potential for nearby Albany, the state capital, since Albany was the Erie's eastern terminus.

So, when the work of building the canal was done and the opening celebration started, with a cavalcade of boats coming all along the new Erie Canal from Buffalo with Governor DeWitt Clinton aboard, Schenectady's residents decided to boycott it. They didn't even go down to the canal banks to watch. The only delegation was a group of students from Union College who felt that someone, at least, ought to acknowledge the great engineering achievement. The students, marching down to the canal in full uniform as the "College Guards," fired a welcoming musket salute to the Governor and his entourage of canal boats.

But as it turned out, Schenectady needn't have worried. By 1829 competition for packetboat trade was so keen along the canal bank in one area that the section became known as "The Battleground." Ticket scalping was as keen there as you might find today outside the Providence Civic Center on a PC Friars home-game evening. It seemed that, after all, none of the Erie's travellers wanted to board the canal boats in Albany, since they would then have to ride Erie water through twenty-seven tedious locks around the Cohoes Falls. It was much more practical (and considerably faster!) to take a stagecoach or horse the quick and straight fifteen miles to Schenectady and get aboard the canal packets there. In time, twenty thousand canal boats a season were streaming into the Dorp's canal basin, one every seventeen minutes, day and night.

Actually, by early 1824 — a good year before the canal officially opened — freight and passenger boats maintained a regular schedule between Schenectady and Rochester to the west. With the completion of the Erie and the increase in passenger travel, Schenectady became one of the most riotous towns in the state. Packet boats became the most popular and profitable operation on the Big Ditch. The packet was far different from the ordinary freight-hauling canal boat. Although some freighters did carry passengers, "the boisterous deportment and unhealthy language of the crew," wrote a Schenectady historian, Chester Woodin, "placed this form of transportation in the class with 'steerage.'"

The packet was a marvel of the day. It was ornamented, painted in bright colors, with flower boxes and awnings to complete the gay decor. Its tiller might be of gold or silver paint. The Erie Canal packet was a floating hotel, offering the same amenities. "The curtained bunks, carpeted floors, neat dining room and kitchen," said Woodin, "completed a picture of compact neatness and comfort yet unknown to the lumbering, dusty and dangerously careening stagecoach travel of the era."

Most of the people who wanted to book passage on the packets came by stagecoach to Schenectady, arriving at a point of what later became Dock Street on the Erie, just south of State Street today. There they were met by a vanguard of "runners" who worked for the packet lines. They were eager to seize a potential passenger, along with his luggage, and to lure him aboard the boat owned by the line they represented.

Sketch of a canal packet boat with passengers on the cabin roof and the steerman signalling by his canaller's horn as the boat approaches a village.

With several companies, each operating four or more packet boats, the competition was understandably keen. An early passenger from Saratoga found his encounter with the runners at Dock Street at harrowing one. Upon arriving in Schenectady, he stepped from his coach to be quickly enveloped, he said, in a circle of runners whose mingled sales pitches frightened him half to death.

"This way, Govnor, *Queen of the Mohawk*, fastest packet on the line," said one. "Light as a feather — she'll have you in Rochester faster than you have a right to expect."

Then the next was heard from. "Ride the *Erie Dreamboat*, squire, feather beds, downy pillows, three square meals a day — for a dollar less than any other boat on the line."

"You'll get three square meals, all right, colonel, of corned beef and cabbage, not square either, but round the clock," countered a third. "Ride with us on the *Dutch Flyer* and slumber

42

in a bed that will lull you to sleep like a babe."

"Slumber? You'll be up half the night chasin' bed bugs!" yelled yet another line's agent. "Get aboard the *Will'O'Wisp* and learn what a good night's sleep is like."

That was enough to stir up a ruckus. With fists flying, the hawker for the *Dutch Flyer* ploughed into the *Will'O'Wisp* man, and the fight was on. The Saratogan reported that everyone in sight joined in — it was anybody's fight. Three participants were pushed into the canal but kept on fighting all the same. Some canallers were jailed, but the battlers earnestly continued the brawl in the lockup.

"Schenectady," said the Saratogan, "richly deserves the title bestowed upon it." He felt it was, indeed, a battlefield.

The oldest part of Schenectady is an area nearest the Mohawk known as the Stockade District, since 1962 protected by the Historic Zoning Ordinance. An underground waterway once flowed beneath the Stockade. This miniature canal with towpath and all was used to transport travelers from the Mohawk River to the Erie Canal. The subway was discovered one morning when a girl whose family lived at 3 Front Street looked out her bedroom window and didn't see her mother's rose garden. When the family investigated, they found that it had fallen into the old underground canal tunnel.

One of the Stockade's notable sons was Joseph Yates, Schenectady's first mayor in 1798 and the seventh governor of the State of New York. His brother, Henry, became a senator from Albany County, and another, Andrew, earned a Doctor of Divinity degree and was one of the first professors at Union College. A fourth brother, John, became a member of Congress from Madison County and was one of the builders of Canada's Welland Canal.

Chapter 9

Bonnets in the Wind

Did you ever lose your hat on a windy day? Wind often whipped in gusts across the Erie Canal where it passed through Schenectady, over what is today's Erie Boulevard. It caused no end of embarrassment to the ladies who crossed over any of the bridges across the canal. When a sudden gust just happened along, it could blow their skirts up to reveal laced petticoats in a most shocking manner for those days!

One time near the turn of the century, a dignified youthful woman walking across the State Street bridge paused to watch the boaters and canal traffic below. She wore very fine clothes, including a swishing brocaded skirt and fine blouse, and she had on a most attractive wide-brimmed blue velvet hat, topped by a black ostrich feather. Beautiful auburn hair showed out from under the hat brim. Suddenly, the tricky canal breeze swept over the bridge, caught up the lady's velvet hat and sailed it high in the air before deposting it in the Erie's water below. But as this was happening, the genteel lady ran pell-mell from the scene. The boaters and dock workers who watched her broke into loud guffaws, for along with that beautiful hat, proud ostrich feather and all, the pesky canal wind had lifted her auburn hair clear off her head, revealing a now wigless, grey-haired older woman.

44

Aqueduct at Rexford, east of Schenectady, on the enlarged Erie Canal.

Chapter 10

Rexford Story

At Rexford, just east of Schenectady, the Erie Canal crossed over the Mohawk River on a long aqueduct. A canaller stopping by McClare's Hotel there one day went into the tavern and bet the barkeeper a dollar he could down a gallon of hard cider without taking more than three breaths. When the hotel's bartender took him up on it, the boater said he would like to leave for few minutes but that he'd be right back.

The boater returned a short time later, and the bartender set out a gallon jug. The canaller wasted no time in giving it a full tilt, and he emptied the contents of the jug with little effort.

He'd won the bet easily, but the bartender was bug-eyed.

"Didn't think it could be done," he told the canaller, shaking his head in doubt over what he had just seen with his own eyes.

The Erie boater wiped his mouth with his sleeve. "T' tell the truth, neither did I," he answered with a satisfied grin, "'til I run down to yer neighbor tavern t' find out.!"

Chapter 11

How to Retrieve "Choppers" from the Erie Canal

Some Erie boaters could tell stories as good as those of any lumberjack from Paul Bunyan country. Over in Troy, New York, for example, they'd tell yarns at the drop of a stovepipe hat.

Some Troy folk recall the time a canal boat pulled up alongside an Erie dock, and the canal cook lost her false teeth overboard. She leaned over the side and tried vainly to fish those teeth out of the water.

The boat's Captain told her that that was no way to find them, so he put a good-sized slice of steak on a fishline and threw it into the canal. The teeth snapped right at it, and he hauled the lost teeth back aboard.

"I knew Susie's teeth couldn't resist a good beefsteak," said the Erie boater.

Chapter 12

Canvass White's Cement

At the time the Erie Canal project began, good hydraulic cement required for lock construction had to be imported from England at great cost in time and money. After some experiments locally, it was demonstrated that a kind of rock near the line of the Erie Canal in Madison County could be converted into a cement equal to the imported product. Finding a native cement in 1817 was a plus indeed for the Erie advocates.

The first works of masonry on the Erie were contracted to be done with common quicklime. Two Madison county contractors by the names of Harris and Livingston agreed to furnish a quantity of the lime for the construction of aqueducts and culverts on the Middle Section between Rome and Salina. When they began to deliver, the purchasers, upon trying it out, found that it would not slack. The matter was much talked about among the construction crews and eventually came to the attention of the project engineers, Canvass White and Benjamin Wright, who set about to investigate.

A scientific gentleman from Herkimer, one Dr. Barto, was called upon to make experiments to see what might be done. He took some of the rough stone, and, in the hammer shop of John B. Yates at Chittenango, he burned a parcel and pulverized it in a mortar, then took it to Elisha Carey's barroom where, in the presence of White, Wright and several others, mixed it with sand, rolled a ball of it, and placed it in a bucket of water for the night. By morning it had set and was found solid enough to roll across the floor.

Dr. Barto pronounced it cement, not inferior to the European kind.

Portrait of Canvass White by Hugh Bridport; gift of William P. White and W. Mansfield White through the Oneida Historical Society.

Canvass White had recently returned from England where he had familiarized himself with the way bridges, canals, aqueducts, and culverts were made and the ingredients of their construction. At considerable personal expense and through repeated experiments, he found the new cement to be an excellent substitute for the European, and he sought and obtained a patent right for a native waterproof cement, which was granted on February 1,

1820. He later devoted much time and effort to further experimentation and to introducing the cement over the doubts and sometimes strong objections of construction workers.

Canvass White was a notable member of the group of pioneer American engineers who received their training on the Erie. He was the grandson of Hugh White, the settler of Whitestown in Oneida County. He first became associated with the Erie project in 1816 and assisted Chief Engineer Benjamin Wright in the early surveys. Late in 1817, with DeWitt Clinton's approval, Canvass White made an extensive trip through Great Britain for the purpose of examining canal construction and bringing back surveying instruments for the canal construction task at home. This experience made Canvass White one of Wright's most valuable assistants and, in time, he was acknowledged as the canal's chief expert in designing locks and their equipment.

White spent some years with the statewide canal project, holding positions on the eastern section, and he supervised the important Glens Falls feeder. In 1825 he succeeded Loammi Baldwin as Chief Engineer of the Union Canal in Pennsylvania, but ill health forced him to give up this position. White later worked on the New York City water supply and the lock at Windsor on the Connecticut River, where the Hartford-Springfield Bradley International Airport is now situated. He was also a consulting engineer for the Schuylkill Navigation Company in Pennsylvania, and he served as Chief Engineer for the Delaware and Raritan Canal in New Jersy and the Lehigh Canal in Pennsylvania.

Chapter 13

The Self-Taught Surveyor

James Geddes lived near the center of the state and all of his interests were connected with the growth and prosperity of the area near Syracuse where he had made his home. As a New York State assemblyman, he pressed untiringly for action to allow the construction of an inland waterway between Lake Erie and the Hudson River.

Born of Scotch ancestry in Carlisle, Pennsylvania, James Geddes moved in 1794 to Onondaga County, New York, where he became one of the pioneers in the salt industry destined to make Salina and Syracuse well known. The nearby town of Geddes was named for him. He was admitted to the bar and became justice of the peace in 1800, then judge of both the county court and the court of common pleas. He was twice elected to the New York State Assembly, in 1804 and again in 1822, and he also served in Washington, D.C. with the Thirteenth Congress, 1813-1815.

Gouverneur Morris, whose lands were far to the west of Geddes's, was earnestly promoting a new transportation system and kept the subject of an inland water route before Simeon DeWitt, the state's Surveyor-General. During Geddes's first term as assemblyman in the state capital, DeWitt talked to him of the possibility of constructing a canal from the Great Lakes to the Hudson River. The idea fascinated Geddes. He visited various sections of the state to secure more information and then launched a campaign to arouse interest in building a canal. Although he had only an elementary education, was entirely without technical training, and had used a surveyor's level only on one previous occasion, he ran the first survey in 1808 under appointment from DeWitt. His report to the Legislature on January 20, 1809, established the fact that it was feasible to construct a canal along a route essentially the same as that later adopted for the Erie Canal. His report also included surveys of routes suggested for canals from Oneida Lake to Lake Ontario, from the Oswego River to Lake Ontario, and from Lake Erie to Lake Ontario around Niagara Falls.

With no civil engineers in the state at the time, this self-taught land surveyor made a remarkable test level from Rome, embracing nearly one hundred miles of leveling. The difference at the junction in the levels, despite his "amateur" status, was less than one and one-half inches!

After serving in the War of 1812, Judge Geddes was engaged by the Canal Commissioners as one of four "principal engineers" to construct the Erie and Champlain canals, tasks to which he devoted himself from 1816 to 1822. In that year he surveyed a canal from the Ohio River to Lake Erie, and in 1827 the federal government secured his services to examine routes for the Chesapeake & Ohio Canal. Subsequently, Geddes performed similar work for canals in Pennsylvania and Maine.

It seems hard to believe that persons with almost no training and little formal education could achieve success in such demanding technical tasks, yet James Geddes is an example of the remarkable people involved in the canal and what they accomplished.

Chapter 14

Professor Eaton's Scientific Expedition

Dr. Sam Rezneck of Rensselaer Polytechnic Institute was fascinated with the history of the early days of the famous engineering school, and he liked especially to tell about the field trips on the Erie Canal that were coincident with both the canal's and Rensselaer's beginnings.

One of the more unusual uses to which the Erie Canal was put in the years immediately following its completion, said Professor Rezneck, was as a convenient route for a travelling school for scientific study and observation. This endeavor was the brainchild of Amos Eaton, founder and first Senior Professor of the Rensselaer School, a pioneer venture in scientific education itself. Established in 1824 under the patronage of Stephen Van Rensselaer, a canal commissioner and last of the Hudson Valley Patroons, this school in Troy, the eastern terminus of the canal, served as a center for the practice and propagation of Eaton's then-novel theories and methods for instructing persons "in the application of science to the common purposes of life."

Both patron and professor were connected with the fulfillment of the Erie Canal project. Van Rensselaer was a member and president of the canal commission appointed in 1810, and Eaton served as his agent in directing a geological and agricultural survey along the canal route during the later years of construction. Eaton had arrived in the area in 1818, opening a new career at the age of forty, after earlier stints in law, land business, and as an itinerant lecturer and ardent advocate of adult and practical education in science. This zeal he had communicated to Van Rensselaer, who announced that his principal object of the new school at Troy was to qualify teachers for instructing the sons and daughters of farmers and mechanics in the application of experimental chemistry, philosophy, and natural history, to agriculture, domestic economy, the arts, and manufactures.

It was a pretty large order in 1824.

The summer tour of study and travel on the Erie Canal was for Eaton a means of broadening the scope of his modest educational system and of publicizing its methods by student participation and demonstration. There were two such ventures, in 1826, and again in 1830, the latter advertised ambitiously for students, teachers, and others as a "Rensselaer School Flotilla"!

Both trips included Asa Fitch in their company. Fitch was a Rensselaer student who recorded his experiences in two volumes of a diary which he kept for many years beginning in 1821 at the age of twelve. Fitch's *Diary* for 1826-27 and 1830 presents the most comprehensive contemporary account of the new education in science, which inspired Fitch and other Rensselaer students to follow careers in science. Asa Fitch himself served for many years as New York's first State Entomologist and won wide recognition for a series of reports on "The Noxious and Other Insects" of the state. His *Diary* is the report of an alert and sensitive young man, who, during the expeditions observed the natural scene, as well as the life of the booming young towns along the canal. At the same time, the *Diary* offers a vivid portrayal of canal travel at an early date, along with keen descriptions of scientific, scenic, and social observations and experiences.

Asa Fitch first met Professor Amos Eaton in April 1826, when he was interviewed for study. Suitably impressed, the lad returned to join the first expedition on April 25, just in time to attend the first commencement exercise at which ten students received Rensselaer degrees. By May 2, the canal boat *Lafayette*, on which the company were to live and work together for several weeks, was ready to depart. The boat was loaded with bedding and baggage, stove, cooking utensils, and crockery. The company included Professor Eaton, two of his sons, former and present students, and several outsiders, among them Joseph Henry, who had recently been appointed professor at the Albany Academy and just beginning his own scientific career.

New York's first State Entomologist, Dr. Asa Fitch, who as a student kept a diary of the Rensselaer scientific expedition on the Erie Canal in 1826.

George W. Clinton, son of DeWitt Clinton and a graduate of Hamilton College, was also aboard. His *Journal* of this expedition is the only other account extant. (Happily, it was reprinted in 1910, thanks to the Buffalo Historical Society.)

With twenty passengers and a crew of four — captain, pilot, cook, and driver — the *Lafayette* was a crowded boat, and its single large cabin had to be used for all purposes. Eaton slept in one corner, on a box in which bed boards were stored during the daytime. At night these "beds" consisted of boards placed across the aisles from benches to lockers. Fitch commented that "this manner of sleeping, after we got a little used to it, was as comfortable to us as the softest bed. I slept very comfortably to-night in the cabin, with only a cushion under me and my chamblet cloak over me." Later, however, some boys decided that it was impossible for the entire party to sleep in the cabin and fitted out a tent on the after-deck. In addition, many found it even more convenient to sleep ashore, at taverns, near where the boat was laid up for a night. Frequently, they left the boat anyway, for purposes of exploration, walking cross country to geological sites, and rejoining the boat as it progressed slowly through locks or over aqueducts.

As the *Lafayette* moved along at its leisurely pace, they took special note of numerous villages along the way: Little Falls, where locks of the old Western Inland Lock Navigation Company, the first around the Falls, were partly demolished; Utica, a merchantile "hubbub of confusion"; Whitesboro, deemed "the most pleasant village of any yet visited"; Oriskany, where Professor Eaton lectured on alluvial formations and the Revolutionary War battle fought there by General Herkimer's troops; Rome, where the students sought to find relicts from Fort Stanwix; Chittenango, with its Polytechny, a school established by John B. Yates to instruct "the laboring classes in Latin, Greek, chemistry, natural history, surveying, and astronomy"; the new village of Syracuse, of which Fitch wrote it was nicely "laid out into streets, and has 3 handsome churches"; Montezuma, notorious for its ague and fever-inducing swamp; Rochester, meeting the later politician Thurlow Weed, then editor and printer of the local newspaper; and finally Tonawanda, the end of the line.

From Tonawanda, they travelled on foot to Niagara Falls before going to Buffalo, where Professor Eaton gave one of his many lectures on the Rensselaer School idea. Students and professor dined at the home of General Peter B. Porter, former Congressman and later Secretary of War, at his extensive estate in Black Rock. The expedition started back east on May 25.

During the trip they had recorded significant aspects of the botany, geology, and entomology of New York State. In addition, Professor Eaton had received from General Porter some choice minerals for his collection, student Asa Fitch had gathered specimens with his bug-net and become initiated into a life-long scientific career, a new village along the route had been given a name (Gasport) as a result of their scientific explorations, and the Rensselaer idea of education had been spread across the state.

Asa Fitch totaled up the cost for himself, a typical student, for boat expenses, entertainment ashore, and miscellaneous items like "pea-nuts," lemonade, a pint of whiskey, and a copy of *Don Juan*, which he purchased in Rochester to read on the canal boat.

His total bill for the trip came to a staggering $48.50!

Chapter 15

Paddy Ryan, Prize-Fighter

Canal boaters and fights often went hand in hand, and the Erie Canal certainly had its share of mayhem-making brawlers and roisterers. Newspapers frequently reported on the fighting and other notorious activities of the boaters, especially at canal terminal points such as Buffalo and Watervliet, and a number of novelists dealing with the canal have managed to include in their fiction a major scrap or two between canal bullies to heighten the action. But would you think that one of the honorable "world champion" prize-fighters started out on the Erie?

He was the great boxer Paddy Ryan, who came over from Ireland a real "Tip" from Tipperary at the tender age of eight. Patrick Henry Ryan was born in 1853 on Saint Patrick's day. Four years after his arrival in Watervliet, New York, he was working as an Erie Canal locktender, and one day he saved a youngster named Judy McGraw from drowning in the canal. That made him a local hero, but more was yet to be heard of Paddy Ryan. He opened a "Sidecut" bar in Watervliet and fought many a battle there and in other Watervliet saloons.

Paddy Ryan loved boxing, and he got his formal training from Jimmy Killoran, athletic director at the Rensselaer Polytechnic Institute, Stephen Van Rensselaer's young engineering college just across the river in Troy. In his prize-fighting bouts and boxing exhibitions, Paddy used to wear green stockings and black trunks ornamented with green shamrocks, with a red-white-and-blue belt thrown in for good measure. He surely was "all American"! When Johnny Dwyer, who claimed to be the American heavyweight champ, gave an exhibition at Troy with the European champion, Joe Goss, Paddy challenged him. Dwyer never showed up for the fight, and Ryan claimed the title by default. In the manner of the day, the Englishman Goss then challenged Ryan.

In June 1880, Paddy Ryan and Joe Goss met in the ring. Staged in West Virginia, the bare-knuckles bout lasted eighty-six rounds, and Paddy Ryan was the winner. As New York's premier folklorist Harold W. Thompson put it, "The King of the Erie Canal was the Champion of the World!"

A scant two years later Paddy Ryan lost his boxing crown. On February 7, 1882, in a match at Mississippi City, Mississippi, that was fought with bare knuckles and on the turf, Ryan was knocked out by the Boston-born John L. Sullivan.

That bout, which ran only nine rounds, was attended by another legendary figure. In the audience was Jesse James.

Chapter 16

Macedon Incident

Fighting seems to have been a tradition on the old canal, and there were a number of memorable ones, to say the least. A fellow whose father lived in Macedon for six years before the turn of the century, liked to talk about one of the biggest, riproaring-est fights that ever occurred on the Erie. His father, he said, called the canal "The Roaring Giddap," and the big fight he recalled happened one day in the spring, only a week or so after traffic opened following the winter lay-up.

It seems that a group of log rafts coming down from Buffalo arrived at the lock at Macedon, a small village on the Erie in the western part of the state. These rafts had to go through lockage five at a time, tied together; even so, they held up boat traffic for miles in either direction, eastbound and westbound. Boaters generally disliked rafters anyway, but this particular tie-up saw an end to all patience.

After 131 canal boats were strung out in line waiting for their turn at the Macedon lock, the Erie boaters rebelled. As the fighting broke out, rafters and boaters had plenty of exercise in the ensuing melee, while the wary locktenders had already "closed shop" and headed off to town to spend their unexpected free time at a local tavern.

According to a local newspaper, when the fighting was finally over, it took two more days and three nights to clear up the damage and get the canal traffic started again through Macedon.

Chapter 17

Irish Tale

Have you ever wondered why there weren't any snakes along the towpath of the Erie Canal? Nineteenth-century New Yorkers took it for granted, and for all we know, the same might be said about the banks of the present New York State Barge Canal. At any rate, canallers will tell you that snakes shied clear of the Old Erie. It seems a skipper named Joe was responsible for ridding the canal towpath of the creatures.

Going along through a school of water snakes on the Erie one time, Captain Joe's boat was carrying a number of Irish immigrants when one of them lost his balance and fell overboard. That Irish fieldhand's dunking gave Joe an idea, especially when he saw how quickly the snakes skeedaddled from around the lad.

Now, the Erie boater knew that all Irish immigrants traditionally carried some field dirt from the old country with them. He also knew all about how the good Saint Patrick had chased the snakes out of Ireland. Putting two and two together, he reasoned that maybe he had a solution to the snake problem. Sure enough, when he sprinkled the towpath with dirt collected from the other Irish passengers aboard his boat, land snakes vanished just like the water varmints had done. So, like Johnny Appleseed with his seedlings, Joe started dotting the Erie towpath with Irish field dirt as he went along the canal.

From the day of that Erie boater's "experiment," few snakes were ever seen along the Erie Canal.

Scene on a canal boat.

Chapter 18

The Story of the
Cleopatra O'Leary

Asa Brown was talking one day to a canaller from up Albion way, and they got to comparing notes about boaters they had known and what they'd heard about the Erie Canal even before their time. Somewhere in the conversation, applejack was mentioned, and that triggered the following recollection in Asa's friend. He had heard it from someone who had lived in Pittsford on the Erie.

It seems a fellow used to have a boat called the *Cleopatra O'Leary* that was built especially to haul grain in bulk. The *Cleopatra O'Leary* was nice and tight and clean, and he'd tied up at Fancher one winter. This is the way he told his story.

There was a farmer in Fancher who'd made up his mind to go into the cider business, and when I got to Fancher he was near crazy. He'd bought tons of apples, and he had them all piled up around his mill, and he was ready to start grinding. But he'd got all his apples before he realized that he didn't have enough barrels to put his cider in. I felt sorry for him, and I told him he could run his cider right into the *Cleopatra O'Leary*. It wasn't far — just a couple of hundred feet — from the mill to the canal bank, and I figured the cider would keep the timbers tight so I wouldn't have to send the boat to the drydock for caulking in the spring. Besides, he told me if I'd let him use the boat I could have all the cider I could drink.

Well, sir, this fellow built a plank flume from the mill to the canal bank, and the cider started to pour in. It came for days and days, until the boat was full right up to the hatches. Then he rented his neighbor's cistern and filled that up with cider, too. Then she started to work, and the foam rolled up over the deck of the *Cleopatra O'Leary* and down into the canal. There wasn't a lot of water left, but there was some, and there was fish in it, too. It was a great sight to see — the big Erie bass and carp staggering up and down the canal, hiccoughing like leaky boilers. All the tom-cats in Fancher gathered around, and they thought the poor soused fish would be easy pickings. But they soon found out different.

A carp, you know, is generally pretty shy and minds its own business, but a carp with a hard-cider hangover is something else again, and they turned the tables and chased the cats. For years after that, the Fancher cats wouldn't even eat canned salmon, they was so nervous about fish.

I rigged up my bilge-pump, and every time I felt thirsty I'd pump myself a basin of cider. It was pretty mild weather all through December, and the cider kept working, and by New Year's it was really strong stuff — good drinking, if you didn't mind the flavor of oakum.

Then the weather dipped. It started to freeze, and how it froze that winter!

Maybe you don't know it, but cider don't freeze solid like water. Cider-ice is sort of slushy, and I wasn't worried about my boat busting from the ice pressure. But my pump kept clogging up, and I kept poking around trying to find a place that wasn't froze, and finally I find it right about in the middle of the boat. You know, it was just the water in that cider that was freezing and forcing the alcohol into the center of the boat, and by the middle of February I was getting 120-proof applejack out of my pump. I never had such a good time as I had that winter. I lived high, too, for I could take a gallon jug of that concentrated cider and swap any farmer around a leg of beef for it or a couple of fat chickens. The farmer who owned the cider was drinking what came out of his neighbor's cistern, and he just couldn't understand how I got so much more fun out of my drinking than he did. Any man that's got any kind of a head for cider can drink maybe a gallon of it, but I couldn't handle more than a quart or two of the stuff out of my boat and feel too perky the next day.

When spring came the owner got some barrels together and started to pump out the boat to run the cider into his barrels. He was going to make a mess of vinegar to sell. By this time, the cider was thawed out again, and I'd drunk most of the power out of my boatload of apple juice, and all he had was some sour water. He just couldn't figure it out — at least he couldn't until the water came into the canal again and I was on my way. Then, when he did find out what had happened, I had to paint a new name on my *Cleopatra O'Leary* and try to go through Fancher after dark.

He might be still waiting for me with a shotgun. Some persons just don't seem to want to show gratitude.

Chapter 19

The Long and Short
of "Long Level"

Canal terms are often hard to pin down as to precise meaning. One especially confusing phrase in the canal boater's vocabulary, for example, is "Long Level." Essentially, the term "long level" referred to a stretch of canal between any two locks at some distance (hence "long") apart. Many nineteenth century travellers wrote in their diaries and books of "the Long Level" (often with capital letters used) on the Erie, and the unwary reader can be confused as to geography.

Construction of the Erie was begun in Rome to take advantage of the naturally level terrain of the state's midsection. That portion of the canal between Utica and Salina (now Syracuse) was planned first because there were no obstacles to construction and the level surface required no locks. In October, 1891, a 98-mile section including this long level between Utica and the Seneca River was completed, and the first boat traveled from Rome to Utica.

The original Long Level (sometimes called "the Rome Level" or "the Utica Level") on Clinton's Ditch ran 69.5 miles from Lock 53 at Frankfort, some eight miles east of Utica, to Lock 54, three-quarters of a mile east of Syracuse. *Gordon's Gazetteer* (1836) refers to this as "the longest canal level in the world."

From Lock 78 at Brighton, a Rochester suburb, the Rochester Level (also called "the Genesee Level") ran sixty-five miles to the combined locks (Locks 79-83) at Lockport.

When the Erie Canal was enlarged, a lock was put in at Utica, and the original Long Level was straightened at several places, reducing its length to fifty-six miles. Twelve miles of kinks were taken out of the 363-mile canal, all told, making the enlarged Erie 351 miles long. The Rochester Level on the enlargement was a shade over sixty-two miles long and hence became the new Long Level, although force of tradition generally meant that the term "Long Level" continued to be used for the Utica-Syracuse run.

Rome on the Long Level

*Tyrone Power, as depicted in J.T. Bowen's
lithograph (1837), in costume for "St. Patrick's
Eve," which the British actor wrote. His visit to
America in 1830 and his tour of upstate New
York are included in a travel book he published
a few years later in England.*

Chapter 20

Tyrone Power's
Erie Canal Mosquitoes

Many notable persons travelled on New York's famed Erie Canal within the first decade or two after it opened, when the Grand Canal was filled with sleek canal packetboats carrying tourists and other passengers across the state. In the 1830's the stream of tourists included such famous persons as Frances Kemble, the actress; Captain Marryat, a successful and very popular English novelist, who made sketches of Buffalo harbour and other scenes for his memoirs; Fanny Trollope, mother of the well known British novelist and an author in her own right, who thought that Trenton Falls, near Utica, was a marvelous sight; and European royalty like Duke Bernhard of Saxe-Weimar.

One of the illustrious contemporary foreign tourists was a Shakespearean actor named Tyrone Power. His descendant, British motion picture actor Tyrone Power, is well known to Hollywood film fans as the romantic hero of such films as "The Mark of Zorro," "Blood and Sand," and other adventurous, swashbuckling screen epics. In the early 1830's, the earlier actor rode the Erie Canal while he was touring the United States. Like so many other European travellers, he felt he had to include New York's new and already internationally acclaimed waterway on his itinerary. Also, like many of his fellow tourists to America, he marveled at the Erie accomplishment while, at the same time, he found canal-boating itself somewhat tedious and disagreeable.

One evening during his trip, when he was aboard an east-bound boat out of Rochester, the mosquitoes began to bite. He had already given up several attempts to fit his robust frame into the sleeping salons' meagre hammocks. He decided it best to remain on deck throughout the night. As he swatted and looked ruefully at the too-plentiful mosquitoes, a canaller told him, "Thim's the real galinippers. Come all the way north for the summer from the Red River. Let a man go to sleep with thim chaps around and if he put his head in a cast-iron kittle, they'd make a water-pot of it by morning!"

The canaller was impressed by Tyrone Power's apparent gullibility.

"Why, they're strong enough to lift a canal boat out of the water," he added, "if only they could get their bills underneath her!"

Whether he believed the boater or not didn't matter. Tyrone Power spent the rest of the night smoking his see-gars on deck, he said, and slapped Erie skeeters until dawn.

Chapter 21

McCarthy's Mules

Now, most folks have seen tightrope walkers at a circus or carnival, but how many do you suppose have seen mules treading a taut line?

It's said that a towpath driver named McCarthy owned some truly remarkable animals. They were ordinary-looking mules, all right, and they did a good job of pulling canal boats up and down the canal. They performed their daily trick well, but there was another "trick" about these canal mules.

McCarthy, you see, had trained 'em special. According to Erie tradition, when mules were changed the canal boat had to come to the bank and stop long enough for the plank "hoss-bridge" to be let down for the fresh mules, or horses as the case might be, to cross over from the boat to the towpath and the tired ones to return to the boat to their stalls. Well, McCarthy trained his mules to save time by marching single file, like tightrope walkers, along the tow rope. It made a great sight, these McCarthy-trained mules, to see two or three of them tripping along a tow rope gracefully as you please.

Chapter 22

A Bag of Bullheads

A Pittsford canaller said it was about 1857 or so, when the bank of the Erie Canal let go in a flood. It happened east of Rochester near Albion, and the farm country along the canal had all its seed washed out. Local farmers lost their wheat crop that year, but they had an awful lot of pike to help make up for it. They came along in wagons and pitch-forked the fish into the wagons by the ton.

A fellow named Johnny O'Brien heard about the break in the canal and started out with a gunny sack over his shoulder to fill up with some loose fish. When he arrived on the scene, however, most of the pike were gone, thanks to the farmers' zeal; but there were thousands of bullheads lying around yet, so Johnny filled his bag with those bullheads. He tossed it over his shoulder, carefree like, and started back to town.

Now, the bullhead fish often went by the name of "stickle-back" in regional parlance, and with good reason. When Johnny O'Brien shouldered his sackful, about forty of the bullheads drove their stingers into him at once, and the yell he let out scared children in villages clear to Syracuse. He lit out along the Erie Canal towpath, nonetheless, and at every step a new bull-head spike would jab into him, and at every jab he'd simply run faster.

People around Albion along the canal, claim that nobody nor nothing ever went faster until the New York Central Railroad's *Empire State Express* came along.

Chapter 23

Joshua the Frog

Empeyville, New York, boasts a famous frog that started out in life as an Erie Canal polliwog. Seems this polliwog was found in the canal in Rome in the 1850's by a fellow named Red McCarthy. When the tadpole turned into frog and settled in the village pond at Empeyville, the villagers noted something strange: he grew bigger and bigger. Pretty soon he had hind legs six feet long and an appetite that devoured chipmunks and sometimes jackrabbits. Every time he jumped into the pond from the shore, the water sprayed thirty feet in the air. They named the frog Joshua, and he gained a fair reputation through the years. He once held a job as a sawman's assistant, for Joshua could haul lumber that was too heavy for the horses.

Just at the turn of the century, Joshua performed one of his most remarkable feats, when the town board asked his help in clearing up an especially dangerous piece of highway which went over Snake Hill. By hooking a chain to one end of the road and giving a mighty tug, Joshua straightened out those Snake Hill curves easily, and in no time at all. Four of Joshua's "grandsons" were reported by the Rome *Sentinel* in 1934 as employed by the city as stump pullers, and other descendants were said to be still inhabiting the Empeyville pond.

Chapter 24

Genesee Aqueduct

Whenever a canal crossed a river or stream, it had to be carried by an aqueduct; and, as everyone knows, there were a good many aqueducts on the Old Erie, eighteen as a matter of fact.

The one which carried the Erie Canal across the Genesee River in Rochester is probably among the most well known, today anyway, because of Rochester's prominence as a city first of flour, and later of cameras and technology and because the Genesee River aqueduct figured importantly in many historical accounts and in literature. The Genesee was commented upon by novelist William Dean Howells in *Their Wedding Journey*. Rochester newspaperman Arch Merrill had many interesting things to say about it in his book, *A River Ramble*. The Genesee got into folklore, too. The legend of Sam Patch is a tale about the famous exhibitionist who performed daredevil feats at Niagara Falls and other perilous places. Sam Patch tried unsuccessfully, however, to make "the fearsome leap" over the Genesee Falls. He died in his attempt on the Genesee in 1829, four years after the Erie Canal opened.

The Erie Canal aqueduct over the Genesee River at Rochester was completed in October 1823. Its design and construction were the achievements of David Stanhope Bates, who had received an appointment from Chief Engineer Benjamin Wright in 1817 as assistant engineer on the middle division of the Erie Canal. The aqueduct Bates designed over the Genesee consisted of nine arches of masonry, of 50-foot span, and two arches over the mill canal of 40-foot span, with a total length of 802 feet.

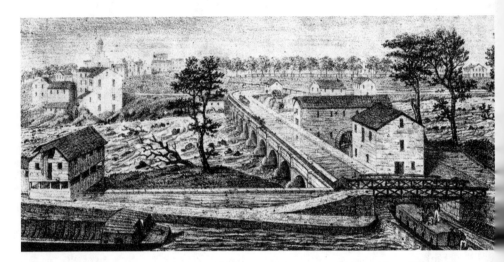

Aqueduct over the Genesee River in Rochester as depicted in a German traveller's account published in Stuttgart in 1835.

Chapter 25

The Strongest Man on the Erie

Once, the Erie was almost dropped into the Genesee River.

Asa Brown's canaller friend complained to him one day. "I understand," he said, "somebody's been telling about me being the Paul Bunyan of the Erie Canal. I don't know much about this Bunyan fellow, except that he appears to be a pretty fair axeman and medium liar." "I'm a truthful man, myself," he admitted gratuitously, "but when I was a boy driving mules I used to hear some pretty tall yarns about canallers." It was then he told about a driver named McCarthy, who was supposed to be the strongest man on the canal back in the forties.

One night, just after he'd had his team pick up the tow-line for his six-hour trick, the rope broke just back of the whiffletree. His mules were fresh and full of oats, and they ran away. McCarthy just picked up the broken end of the line, put it over his shoulder and hauled that boat for five hours, looking for those mules, and nobody else on the canal boat knew what had happened. After about two hours the boat — which was a leaky old tub anyway, and filled with crushed stone — had the bottom ripped out of her on some sunken rock. It sank, but McCarthy never stopped pulling. He hauled that boat along the canal channel for seven more miles, while the boat kept sinking deeper and deeper in the mud.

As luck would have it, the moon came out just before he got to the aqueduct that carried the canal over the river at Rochester, or he'd have ripped the floor of the aqueduct right out and let the canal drop clear into the Genesee River. Mind you, he was headed west, so he was pulling against the current, too.

Anyway, the State Legislature thought he had done a right nice job. They voted McCarthy $500 for scooping the mud out and deepening the canal from Pittsford to Rochester.

Another time, he was invited to a dance. Well, everybody over Pittsford way knew how much he loved to dance, so it was no surprise that when the boys and girls at Knowlesville were having a dance, they told him to be sure to come. He was at Spencerport, heading back towards Knowlesville, when he got word that the village hall had burned down and the dance was off. But the Erie boater wasn't about to let a fire stop him or those kids. Since he had a flat-bottomed boat, he took enough paving blocks aboard to weigh the boat down so it was just scraping canal bottom. Then he hitched his fastest mules to the boat, and they came flying up the canal. When he got to Knowlesville, he unloaded the paving blocks and heaved the boat over, bottom-side up, right against the bank.

The sand and mud in the bottom of the canal had smoothed off the rough planks of the boat and the timbers were as smooth as glass. When they dried off a bit, the Erieman waxed 'em, and the youngsters had their dance after all, on the underside of the canal boat.

Chapter 26

Ballads and Songs

The Erie Canal, the pride of the State of New York, found its way early into the songs of the people who worked on it or dwelt along the towpath. The early canallers sang for reasons easily understood. Singing was a means of entertainment and a release from the monotony and hard life. Breaking into song was a trait of the pioneer, and the canawlers were a convivial, brawling pioneer people. They drank deeply, they ate heartily, they fought eagerly, and they sang lustily. That much of their material had a nautical flavour stems perhaps from one-tenth conscious hyperbole and nine-tenths from sheer pride in boatin' on the Grand Western Canal — the longest and finest inland water communication in the world.

Erie balladry is richly laden with the lore of the times. It speaks for itself. Here are a few tuneful examples of what New York songster Frank Warner liked to call "odd bits," right good samples for a "Canaller's Songbag."

PADDY ON THE CANAL

When at night, we all rest from our labor,
   Be sure, but our rent is all paid,
We laid down our pick, and our shovel,
   Likewise, our axe, and our spade,
We all set a joking together;
   There was nothing our minds to enthral,
If happiness be in this wide world,
   I am sure it is on the canal.

I'M AFLOAT

I'm afloat! I'm afloat! On the E-ri Canawl,
   Its wave is my home, and my scow beats them all—
Off! up with your hats! give three cheers! now three more!
   I'm afloat! I'm afloat! After four months on shore.
I fear not for breakers, I heed not the wave,
   I've the towpath to steer by, and a boat-hook to save;
And ne'er as a lubberly landsman I'll quail,
   When the Captain gives orders to "take in all sail."
Come, boy! Whip the mare! Keep her head to the wind,
   And I warrant we'll soon leave the snails all behind—
Up! Up! with your caps! Now give cheers three times three!
   I'm afloat! I'm afloat!

THE SONG OF THE WOLVERINES

Then there's the State of New York where some are very rich;
Themselves and a few others have dug a mighty ditch
To render it more easy for us to find the way
And sail upon the waters to Michigania,—
Yea, yea, yea, to Michigania.

SONG OF THE CANAL

We are digging the Ditch through the mire;
Through the mud and the slime and the mire, by heck!
And the mud is our principal hire;
Up our pants, in our shirts, down our neck, by heck!
We are digging the Ditch through the gravel,
So the people and freight can travel.

LIFE ON THE CANAWL

A life on the raging canawl,
  A home on its muddy deep,
Where through summer, spring and fall,
  The frogs their vigils keep.
Like a fish on the hook I pine,
  On this dull unchanging shore—
Oh give me the packet line,
  And the muddy canawl's dull roar.

*Broadside of the popular ballad, "Raging Canal," versions of which appeared
as early as the 1840s.*

RAGING CANAL

Come listen to my story, ye landsmen, one and all,
And I'll sing to you the dangers of that raging Canal;
For I am one of many who expects a watery grave,
For I've been at the mercies of the winds and the waves.

I left Albany harbor about the break of day,
If rightly I remember 'twas the second day of May;
We trusted to our driver, altho' he was but small,
Yet he knew all the windings of that raging canal.

It seemed as if the Devil had work in hand that night,
For our oil it was all gone, and our lamps they gave no light,
The clouds began to gather, and the rain began to fall,
And I wished myself off of that raging Canal.

The Captain told the driver to hurry with all speed—
And his orders were obeyed, for he soon cracked up his lead;
With the fastest kind of towing we allowed by twelve o'clock,
We should be in old Schnectedy right bang against the dock.

But sad was the fate of our poor devoted bark,
For the rain kept a pouring faster, and the night it grew more dark;
The horses gave a stumble, and the driver gave a squall,
And they tumbled head and heels into that raging Canal.

The Captain came on deck, with a voice so clear and sound,
Crying cut the horses loose, my boys, or I swear we'll all be drowned;
The driver paddled to the shore, altho' he was but small,
While the horses sank to rise no more in that raging Canal.

The Cook she wrung her hands, and she came upon the deck,
Saying, alas! what will become of us, our boat it is a wreck!
The steersman laid her over, for he was a man of sense,
When the bowsman jumped ashore, he lashed her to the fence.

We had a load of Dutch, and we stowed them in the Hole,
They were not the least concerned about the welfare of their soul;
The Captain went below and implored them for to pray,
But the only answer he could get was, Nix come Ruse, nis fis staa!

The Captain came on deck with a spy glass in his hand,
But the night it was so dark he could not diskiver land;
He said to us with a faltering voice, while tears began to fall,
Prepare to meet your death, my boys, this night on the canal.

The Cook she being kind-hearted, she loaned us an old dress,
Which we raised upon a setting-pole as a signal of distress;
We agreed with restoration, aboard the boat to bide,
And never quit her deck whilst a plank hung to her side.

It was our good fortune, about the break of day,
The storm it did abate, and a boat came by that way.
Our signal was discovered, and they hove along side,
And we all jumped aboard and for Buffalo did ride.

I landed in Buffalo about twelve o'clock,
The first place I went to was down to the dock;
I wanted to go up the lake, but it looked rather squally,
When along came Fred Emmons and his friend Billy Bally.

Says Fred how do you do, and whar have you been so long?
Says I, for the last fortnight I've been on the canal,
For it stormed all the time, and thar was the devil to pay,
When we got in Tonanwandy Creek, we thar was cast away.

Now, says Fred, let me tell you how to manage wind and weather,
In a storm hug to the tow-path, and then lay feather to feather,
And when the weather is bad, and the wind it blows a gale,
Just jump ashore, knock down a horse—that's taking in the sail.

And if you wish to see both sides of the canal,
To steer your course to Buffalo, and that right true and well,
And should it be so foggy that you cannot see the track,
Just call the driver aboard and hitch a lantern on his back.

A TRIP ON THE ERIE
(as sung by Frank Warner)

Chapter 27

Tin Pan Alley Erie

Everyone has heard of the Erie Canal song with its "Low bridge, everybody down" refrain. The song had a number of antecedants, including an old vaudeville tune, that helped pave the way for the now famous Tin Pan Alley song. In the 1880's, when Edward Harrigan produced his new vaudeville comedy, *The Grip*, one of his show tunes was called "Oh! Dat Low Bridge!" A copy of the minstrel number uncovered in the Grosvenor Reference Library in Buffalo begins with these words:

> It's many miles to Buffalo
> Oh, dat low bridge!
> Balky mule he travel slow
> Oh, dat low bridge!

The song most people are familiar with was published by a Tin Pan Alley songwriter, Thomas S. Allen. He called it "Low Bridge, Everybody Down," with the subtitile of "Fifteen Years on the Erie Canal." This tune memorialized the canalboat mule at a time when the Old Erie had given way to the new Barge Canal System that made animal power a thing of the past.

Here's the way Allen began his song:

I've got an old mule and her name is Sal,
Fifteen years on the Erie Canal.
She's a good old worker and a good old pal,
Fifteen years on the Erie Canal.
We've hauled some barges in our day,
Filled with lumber, coal and hay,
And ev'ry inch of the way I know,
From Albany to Buffalo.

Don't be surprised if, even today, you hear some version or variation of "The Erie Canal song." It crops up almost whatever part of the land you might be in. As one of the verses goes,

Oh, every band will play it soon,
Darned fool words and darned fool tune;
You'll hear it sung everywhere you go,
From Mexico to Buffalo.

Chapter 28

Mark Twain's Erie Canal

Every school girl and boy knows of Mark Twain's Huckleberry Finn and Tom Sawyer, and many people remember with amusement his famous short story about the "Celebrated Jumping Frog of Calaveras County." But most folks don't generally connect the great midwestern humourist with New York State and the Erie Canal.

Mark Twain — or Samuel Clemens, if you prefer his real name — did, however, spend some time in Buffalo, New York, writing newspaper sketches for the Buffalo *Courier* there; and the Mark Twain house on the campus of Elmira College is an interesting tourist attraction to visitors to the state's Southern Tier. Twain was taken considerably by the Old Erie, too. When he heard the old canal ballad "The Raging Canal," a traditional and well-known song of the times, he decided to make up a version of his own. He called his "The Aged Pilot Man," and he said he thought it was "one of the noblest poems of the age" when he wrote it.

In the folk memory Twain's literary piece and the traditional ballad often seem to have merged. Twain's poem, which appears in *Roughing It*, is as delightfully "mock heroic" as the older folk song. The poem tells of a stormy night aboard a canal boat on the

"Shortening Sail," an illustration in Mark Twain's Roughing It, for the author's parody verse of life on the raging Erie Canal.

raging Ee-rye-ee when the boat is about to be swamped by wind and wave, and everyone onboard is sure to drown.

> On the Erie Canal, it was
>   All on a summer's day,
> I sailed forth with my parents
>   Far away to Albany.
>
> From out the clouds at noon that day
>   There came a dreadful storm,
> That piled the billows high about,
>   And filled us with alarm.
>
> Our captain cast one glance astern,
>   Then forward glanced he,
> And said, "My wife and little one
>   I never more shall see."
>
> Said Dollinger the pilot man,
>   In noble words, but few,—
> "Fear not, but lean on Dollinger,
>   And he will fetch you through."

Dollinger the pilot man does indeed fetch the canal boat through, but not before the tempest-tossed craft has had to "lighten ship" (on a canal four feet deep!) by ordering cargo thrown over the side.

This is what Mark Twain's canallers got rid of on that hectic trip:

> So overboard a keg of nails
>   And anvils three we threw
> Likewise four bales of gunny-sacks
>   Two hundred pounds of glue
>
> Two sacks of corn, four ditto wheat
>   A box of books, a cow
> A violin, Lord Byron's works
>   A rip-saw and a sow.

Certainly, this was one of the more intriguing cargoes ever to ride Erie water!

Chapter 29

Canal Victuals

No one could accuse our forefathers of not having hearty appetites. Here is a virtual smorgasboard offered by one boater sailing Erie water which saw his passengers "sufficiently victualled" to appease their hunger:

> . . . a pike or bass, fresh caught upon my overnight trawl line; a steak, bacon, sausage, and ham; a platter of scrambled eggs; baked pritties, boiled cabbage and squash; bread, both corn and white; pancakes, both wheat and buck-wheat, with sorghum, maple or honey to choice; and, to wash all down, coffee, tea, milk, skimmigig, and cider.

This, believe it or not, was *breakfast*!

"Dinner," a satisfied passenger observed, "will be heartier."

Tourists to our shores seemed constantly amazed at both the appetites and varieties of fare. "An American breakfast is something astonishing," said Frederick Gerstaecker, a sportswriter of sorts from Germany who toured the country in the 1840's. "Europeans behold in surprise," he observed as he sat down to breakfast one morning on a westbound Erie packet, "coffee, pork, pickled gherkins, potatoes, turnips, eggs, bread, butter, and cheese, all on the table at once." He admitted that it was, however, much more suiting "a hungry Christian" than paler European fare.

Breakfast (or dinner) for packetboat passengers was one thing; meals for the crew, especially on the freight boats, was another. A cured meat product that never graced the tourist's table on a posh packetboat was known as "Black Rock Pork," named after the town just north of Buffalo, and it appears to have been a staple of the canal diet. Here and there, it crept into the boaters' nineteenth century songs, one of which paid homage, as it were, to this product. Here are a few verses to allow you to savor the delicacy:

> I shipped aboard of a lumber-boat,
> Her name was *Charles O'Rourke*.
> The very first thing they rolled aboard
> Was a barrel of Black Rock pork.

> They fried a chunk for breakfast
> And a chunk for luncheon, too.
> It didn't taste so goody-good,
> And it was hard to chew.

> From Buffalo to old New York
> They fed it dear-old-me;
> They boiled the barrel and rest of the pork,
> And we had it all for tea.

Black Rock Pork as part of the canalman's diet found its way into other canal songs, added testimony to the currency of this item of canal fare. This "Canalman's Farewell" was remembered by a Fort Plain resident:

> When I die, lay me on a canal boat
> With my feet toward the bow:
> Let it be a Lockport Laker,
> Or a Tonawanda scow.
> Put forty pounds of Black Rock pork
> Upon my brawny breast,
> And telephone over to the cook
> The driver's gone to rest.

When German nobility visited New York State, they were as

91

impressed as other travellers with the gastronomic wonders on and off the canal. Like his countryman Gerstaecker, Duke Bernhard of Saxe-Weimar-Eisenbach found the food suited his palate. Commenting upon dinner in a canal town tavern, the German traveller wrote that one finds upon a table "beef-steaks, mutton, broiled chicken, or other fowls, fish, and boiled potatoes, which are of a very superior quality." And this was in the 1820's.

If Erie boaters in the old days were enthusiastic about their victuals and prized their eats, in the twentieth century some of their descendants seemed to like to carry on the tradition. In the 1930's a group of canal buffs in the Rochester and Albion area organized the "Society of the Erie Canal," and one of the Society's get-togethers offered a unique and memorable menu. For a meeting in Albion, there were a goodly number of dinner items to satisfy the most voracious appetite and discriminating canawler of 1930.

The menu deserves a respected place in the annals of culinary lore.

The Society of the Erie Canal, for all its potential, quickly passed into history — or folklore perhaps might be more accurate. Its members tried to revivify the days of the Erie, and in the short time the organization existed they turned out some canal-based yarns that would do any Tall Tale Tellers Club proud. Their menu (shown on the next page) also indicates that the Society members had a flare for describing canal victuals as well.

MENU

Fruit Cup *"Holy Farmer Flats"*

Horsetail Soup

Prime Ribs *de Mule Team*

Towpath Potatoes   *"Hoggie"* Sauce

East Dock Squash

Swing Bridge Salad

Packet Line Ice Cream   *"Mudport"* Coffee

Old Towrope Cigars

Chapter 30

Canalboat Sal

The cook, she's a daisy;
   She's dead gone on me.
She has fiery red hair;
   And she's sweet twenty-three.

She's cross-eyed and freckled;
   She's a darling and a pet.
And we use her for a headlight
   At night on the deck.

The tradition of hiring on women cooks aboard Erie boats evoked sufficient response in the canallers to give rise to lines like those above. For whatever reason, the stereotype was developed of a canal cook with bright red hair; perhaps in contrast to the otherwise drab surroundings of canalboat life, this fiery-haired girl formed a part of the boater's romantic ideal. We can guess that some of it is folklore and some of it derives from literature, from modern stories written about the Erie. Much popular knowledge about boaters, cooks, and others who worked the canal probably stems more from writers like Walter D. Edmonds and Samuel Hopkins Adams than from remembered folk tradition. As far as the canal cook is concerned, Edmonds certainly put the capstone on the idea of a red-headed cook named Sal.

Edmonds's canalboat cooks were secured through an employment service, Lucy Cashdollar's Cooks Agency for Bachelor Boaters, that plays a fairly prominent role in his novel *Rome Haul*. Edmonds introduced Sal in a song which is a version of the Thomas Allen canal song, "Low Bridge, Everybody Down," and it may also be that most people now think of Edmonds's song instead of the other one, when they hum the tune. It went like this:

> Drop a tear for Big-foot Sal,
> The best damn cook on the Erie Canal;
> She aimed for Heaven but she went to Hell—
> Fifteen years on the Erie Canal.
>
> The missioner said she died in sin;
> Hennery said it was too much gin:
> There weren't no bar where she hadn't been,
> From Albany to Buffalo.

In verses sung in Buffalo's Bonny Theater in the 1870's, the canalboater's cook had, if not the big feet suggested by the epithet for Walter D. Edmonds's Sal, other enormous, if perhaps slightly undesireable features:

> The cook we had upon the deck
> Stood six feet in her socks;
> Her hand was like an elephant's ear,
> Her breath would open the locks.

This vaudevillian's canalboat cook was a "maid of sixty summers" — perhaps playing on the words of the earlier folksong with its youthful girl of twenty-three. And she was, alas, nameless.

Chapter 31

Johnny Darling Finds a Wife

Catskill Johnny Darling seems to have been involved with the redheaded lady of the canal, too.

Everyone knows that John Caesar Cicero Darling and the mountains he loved were inseparable, but every now and then one of America's folk heroes gets transplanted, as it were, and so it may not be so strange that upstate writer Carl Carmer, another Hamilton College alumnus who liked to work the native soil, literarily speaking, recorded a Darling tale set beyond the mountains where Rip Van Winkle once heard the ninepins roll. Whether the folk hero really went into canal country or not is a moot question. He may have gone, or he may not have. Johnny Darling, himself, was a real storyteller, one of the best. Like Mike Fink and Davy Crockett and a bunch of other Americans. Moritz Jagendorf, who was a story teller in his own right and whose home on Riverside Drive in New York City once hosted wine-and-cheese parties that made the annual midwinter meetings of the New York Folklore Society a gourmet's Mecca, called John Darling "a sandy-whiskered Rip Van Winkle, ragged but undefeated, brandishing his famous magic stick and snickering over his next majestic whopper." Reason enough why John Darling is sometimes called the American Baron Munchausen.

But back to Johnny and Erie Sal. It happened this way.

Johnny had himself a canal boat, aptly named *Erie Queen*, and a cook named Sal. She had flaming red hair, too, and Johnny fell in love with Sal and wanted to marry her. But she decided to make a fishing contest out of it, and said she'd marry whoever caught the most fish, midnight to midnight. Johnny took up the challenge, because that's what folk heroes do.

They were up at Oak Orchard Creek and Johnny had heard all about how great the bass were in those parts, how they'd practically jump into a fisherman's boat. But after a full day sitting in a rowboat, watching the fish jumping all about but getting nairy a bite to haul in, Johnny Darling became pretty discouraged. The fish were running so big and so plentiful he could see schools of those bass run right past his boat, mocking like. When Sal found him near sunset with no fish, she felt sorry for him because, truthfully, she really favored Johnny and wanted him to win. Then he had an idea.

Johnny got a school of the biggest bass between the *Erie Queen* and the shoreline and then, of a sudden, told Sal to put her head down, quick, to the water. Well, sir, that flaming red hair of Sal's scairt those bass so much they leapt out of the water right smack into Johnny's boat as fast as they could wiggle their fins! Before he was done, he'd managed to get over two hundred of Oak Orchard's finest bass into his boat. And that won him the contest — and a bride. Johnny Darling and Redhead Sal were married the next day and honeymooned up the Erie Canal to Tonawanda and Niagara Falls.

Chapter 32

Whales on the Erie

A fellow named Oakes Anderson exhibited a whale on the Erie Canal back in the 1880's. Anderson was a tugboat operator who ran into the whale crossing New York harbor. With Yorker enterprise, he decided he'd take the whale up the Hudson River and onto the Erie. His whale was one of several, apparently, to make the trip, for there are notices of such whale exhibits to be found in broadsides and handbills that were the advertisements of the day.

Probably the best known whale on the Erie is Walt Edmonds's "Cashalot." Edmonds tells many a good tale of the canal days, and this writer of yarns and historical novels grew up in Black River country, near the Black River Canal, which passed the Edmonds's farm at Boonville in the North Country and joined the Erie at Rome, New York. His story has all the earmarks of a good folktale.

Uncle Ben Meekum, it seems, was a canaller living a pretty henpecked existence with his good spouse, Aunt Em. Ben and his driver, Henry Plat, worked the boat and tended the mules, but inside Em ruled the roost. She took pride in their boat, however, and gave it curtained windows and the best geraniums on the Erie. When Em had to visit her ailing Ma, Ben was left to

DON'T FAIL TO SEE THE
LARGEST WHALE
Ever Captured on the American Coast.

WILL BE ON EXHIBITION

On the Canal by Gleason's Knitting Mill, near Ovid St. Bridge,

In Seneca Falls, Monday & Tuesday, Nov. 10 & 11.

THIS MAMMOTH WHALE was captured by Capt. Nickerson, June 5th, 1888, off Cape Ood, 15 miles from shore, 100 miles from Boston, shot with a boom lance, weighed 75 tons, and was 65 feet long. It took 1,500 gallons of fluid to embalm this huge amount of flesh, at a cost of $3,000. You must consider the monstrous size of this animal, when his Tongue Weighed 3,500 Pounds and made 120 Gallons of Oil. His Lower Jaw will seat 25 persons. His Mouth has been fitted up as a Reception Room. A person six feet tall can stand erect in his Mouth, between the Monster's Jaws. We have had 25 young ladies and their teacher in his Mouth, all at the same time; also seen 12 gentlemen seated in his Mouth, enjoying an oyster supper. His Whaleship has been on Exhibition over Two Years, in the Principal Cities of Seven States, and Viewed by Hundreds of Thousands of Astonished People. It is not only a Wonderful Sight, but instructive to Men, Women and Children. The Captain and his Aides will instruct you of the Different Species; how they are captured; show you the Ancient and Modern Weapons used to capture them. Go and see for yourself, and if you find this is not a real Whale, we will cheerfully refund your money.

On Exhibition from 9 A. M. Until 10 P. M. Daily.
ADMISSION, - 15c.   CHIDLREN, - 10c.

Handbill of the 1880's, typical of advertisements for exhibits and shows along the Erie Canal.

A.H. Barben, Seneca Falls

freight alone down to New York City. That proved to be a dramatic turning point in the canal boater's life, beginning when Ben's boat struck a whale in New York harbor.

"What," says Henry Plat to Ben, "are you going to do with a dead whale?" And the driver reminded Uncle Ben that his wife would surely "squeak him good" when she returned and heard about what he had been doing.

"Em," says Uncle Ben, "hasn't got anything to say about my whale."

Then he explained to Henry how he planned to load the whale aboard the *Louisa* and take her up the Erie Canal.

Well, the whale was hoisted onboard the canal boat with her nose on the cabin roof and her tail hanging over the bow. The innards were dug out to allow for a bar and refreshment parlor. When she was full-rigged, the *Louisa* made quite a spectacle going up the canal, with a big sign that said CASHALOT in green letters, and underneath it "Be a Jonah for fifty cents." Ben even put a pair of glasses on the whale. He'd picked them up in an oculist's shop.

By the time the *Louisa* reached Rome, he's made more than a thousand dollars. Farmers came from fifty miles around to see Ben's whale. But as the weather got warmer that summer the whale began to smell. Ben had to keep trimming it in order to get under the Erie's low bridges. As he trimmed the whale, his admission price got smaller, too. By the time Aunt Em returned, though, Ben had taken enough in receipts so that even she had to admit he was quite an entrepreneur, and she looked up to him now as a heroic figure of a man. Ben sold the whale, what was left of it, for fertilizer, and he and Aunt Em led a happy life on their geranium-studded canal boat, *Louisa*.

Chapter 33

Corn and Clover

The Canal Commissioners surely had an inventive bent, when you think about it. Take the canal corn lot, for instance. The state commissioners, said a man from Pittsford on the Erie Canal, got the idea one year that there was a lot of land being wasted along the towpath that ought to be producing crops. So they brought the big fleet owners together, and the first four or five boats out of Buffalo that spring took ploughs, and each ploughed one furrow as the mules dragged the boat along, on the far side of the towpath. They ploughed a narrow strip of land from near Buffalo right down to Albany, and then the next few boats took the job of rolling it, and harrowing it, and then they hitched up one of the new patent seeders and sowed two rows of corn from one end of the canal to the other.

Every once in a while the State would send a cultivator along, and the rows of corn were fertilized with mule manure, so they grew up tall and handsome. The farmers all through the area got kind of mad, claiming the state was maybe competing with them for the corn market, and there was talk of trampling down the whole canal corn lot. But with a boat on the canal about every half mile or so then, they could keep watch all along the line. After a few run-ins with the more irate farmers, things quieted down and there wasn't any more trouble. It was such a bother harvesting the corn, though, that it was never tried again, because a man can't properly drive his mules and shuck corn and toss it over into the boat at the same time.

After that, it was decided to plant clover along the canal, and the state sent every skipper a bag of clover seed. The boaters mixed the seed with the feed for the mules, and they used to clean out the stalls and toss a forkful of manure over on the bank, or heave mule-balls at any cranky farmer they'd spot along the canal. A clover seed, you know, is so tough it can go through a mule's bowels without hurting it any, and they's why the Erie Canal always had a lot of nice sweet clover growing along the banks.

That was one good deed the boaters did for the farmers that seems never to have been fully appreciated. For more'n fifty years their bees gathered honey from those canalbank clover flowers, and none of them realized when they smeared honey on their pancakes how much they owed to those mule-digested clover seeds.

Chapter 34

How Gasport Got Its Name

Villages and towns along the route of the Erie reflected the fact that their existence was tied, economically and geographically, with the noble enterprise. Thus, the "port" names of Lockport, Fairport, Gasport, Newport, and Middleport, reflected the marine aspect of things, and those of a number of other villages were similarly derived naturally from the setting in which they were founded or grew to bustling maturity when the canal opened. Samuel Hopkins Adams, whose forebearers worked the Grand Canal (Adams Basin on the canal was named after one of them), chose the title *Canal Town* for one of his novels, which had as its principal setting the Erie Canal village of Palmyra.

Actually there was a town named "Canal." Probably one of the most appropriately named towns of all during the Canal Era was Canal, New York, which was established as a post office on January 15, 1830. It occurred on the same day the office at Ionia, a short mile north was discontinued. Early settlers had expected "Iony" to be the business and social center of the town of Van Buren, but like other villages just off the line of the Erie Canal, her early promise was not realized.

Canal, New York, lasted onomastically and philatelically for thirty years. It became Memphis in 1860.

One of the towns along the route of the Erie Canal got its name from a professor of science and his group of students. It happened during Professor Amos Eaton's scientific expedition, when he took students from the Rensselaer School (Rensselaer Polytechnic Institute today) on a field trip up the canal from Troy to Tonawanda in 1826.

When their canal boat, the *Lafayette*, was some six miles east of Lockport, Professor Eaton and his companions were able to put their scientific knowledge to practical use. Here they discovered a spring spurting in a basin, which emitted (according to Asa Fitch's *Diary* of the trip) "Carburetted Hydrogen or Coal Gas," the kind which commonly arises from "beds of cole [sic]." When a lighted candle was applied to the bubbling gas, it produced a red flame.

As a result of this discovery, they recommended that the place be named "Gasport," and the proprietor promised to use this name for the settlement just developing there. It is Gasport to this day, and there's now a canalside park, developed right beside the Erie Barge Canal, where you can watch modern canal boats and pleasure craft while picnicking on a summer's day.

Chapter 35

The Thirsty Palmyra Squash

Asa Brown's canal friend from Albion remembered the big drought in western New York a couple of years before the Civil War. It got so hot all the Lake Erie water and all the feeders along the Erie couldn't keep the canal from going dry. Constables had to keep a tight rein. A Weedsport woman was arrested for stranding fifteen canal boats when she filled her washtub from the canal. It was so dry that the Canal Commissioners' towpath walkers went along the canal all summer cutting weeds and grapevines so their roots couldn't suck any water out of the prism. They carried shotguns to shoot at any crows that tried to drink Erie water.

The farmers never paid the canal officials any mind, anyway, and they'd dig up their plants, their beans, corn and pumpkins and dip the roots in the canal water. One fellow from over Palmyra way had a squash vine that he'd been nursing along by spitting on it every few days, and it had two or three nubbins of squash on it when he dragged it over and stuck the roots into the Erie. That vine was so thirsty that it sucked out the water like a big hose and left ten miles of canal bottom bare.

Then the squash started to grow fast as you might blow up rubber balloons, and the farmer had to run like the dickens to keep ahead of them as they swelled up. When a section of vine went past him going like a racer snake, he grabbed at a flower bud, but the bud turned into a flower and then into a good-sized squash so quickly it blew his hand right off as if he'd held a fistful of gunpowder.

He did all right, though. For years afterward, he made a living by peddling sections of stems from the leaves of that renowned Erie-nurtured squash vine. They made good drainage tile.

Palmyra on the Erie

Chapter 36

The "Barbary Coast" Saloons

During the Erie's heyday, West Troy or Watervliet came to be known as "The Barbary Coast of the East." The notorious area near the canal has been compared, because of all its brawling, to the frontier times in the Klondike and Dawson City. The village of Watervliet is just across the Hudson River from Troy, which was itself famous as "the Collar City" and the site of much boat building and other activities associated with the canal.

Here is where the Erie Canal first met the Hudson River and, since it was in many respects the practical (if not actual) terminus of the canal, it was here in Watervliet, after the boats had descended the final locks around the Cohoes Falls, that the boaters who had hired on, along with the drivers and steersmen, were paid their wages for the eastbound trip. Within a two-block area in Watervliet, 23rd Street to 25th Street, there were once twenty-nine saloons, with more around the corner on Union Street. One widow woman owned an entire block and had six different saloons in one building; and Jake Barns, her bartender, had quite a task trying to keep an eye on them all.

The saloons catered to the tour-weary canallers with their pockets filled with ready cash. Some establishments were drinking places, some gambling houses. Some, it was said, were worse.

Many of the saloons had names to match their rough-and-tumble character and that of the clientele. One was Charles Connell's BLACK RAG, another Bill Armstrong's TUB OF BLOOD. Some names sounded gentle enough, like THE PIG'S EAR, THE NEWARK HOUSE, ROCKAWAY BEACH HOUSE, and FREE AND EASY, but these names belied the rambunctuous character of the establishments. Sam Scullen ran a place called PEG LEG HOUSE, which gained even more notoriety when a murder took place there. It seems that a patron named Bill Cronk killed another customer, Bill Donahue, with a whiffletree!

There were places with less violent names as well, however. There was an ARBOR HOUSE, for instance; and a pair of co-proprietors named Rowe and Lang advertised their spirits and hospitality at the disarmingly sober-sounding sign of THE FRIENDLY INN. Another Watervliet tavernkeep named Peter McCarthy ran THE BANK, which may well have taken in more cash than the financial institutions bearing the name.

Chapter 37

Dunkings Around The Dorp

In the 1850's, nine city streets and a railroad crossed the Erie Canal in Schenectady in a network of bridges. One section between Washington Avenue and State Street, referred to locally as the city's harbor, teemed with canallers and townsfolk coming and going in its numerous feed and grain stores, harness shops, hardware stores, warehouses, and stables. In time, many of these buildings, especially along Dock street, took on a less than romantic appearance, typical of sections in most American cities that were adjacent to canal or railroad. In other ways, too, this canal area of Schenectady was typical of canal towns in both New York State and other parts of the country. For one thing, there were always the dunking "incidents."

If the canalside area of West Troy's infamous Sidecut was correctly characterized by "a hundred fights a day, a body a week found in the canal," as Troy journalists put it, Schenectady's Dock Street and "harbor" area couldn't have been too different. As if the so-called Battlefield, where ticket scalpers operated with vocal and physical abandon, wasn't enough, there were the almost constant dunkings. Winter and summer, says county historian Larry Hart, "scarcely a day passed without an incident (or accident) along the canal in this area," with horses, wagons

109

and people falling into the canal quite regularly.

The dunkings, Hart relates, usually were by accident, but sometimes Dock Street ruffians settled their arguments by the "wet or dry method." The rules were simple. In a fight, the person who got thrown into the canal was wrong, and the one who stayed dry was right.

Occurrences filled the local news columns. A horse and cart belonging to the Brownell Coal Company backed off the company dock one day in 1859. The horse was saved from drowning only after its harness was cut. The same night, a span of horses fell into the canal from the towpath opposite Dock Street, and a boy got drawn in with the horses. The lad was rescued by a man who jumped in after him. The horses, noted the local press, were also saved.

One morning, a canal boat driver was roped into the canal between Freeman's Bridge and Schenectady. He floundered about in the water for a while and finally regained the towpath. He was headed for Troy, and he resumed his journey singing "Jordan is a hard road to travel." Another time a grain boat was making fast to the dock near Two Mile House when a rope line accidentally coiled around the leg of a deck hand. The resulting tension, as the canal boat hove to, just about sliced the man's limb in two. He was carried into the hotel and given a good supply of spirits until the doctor came to complete the amputation.

Not all dunkings were the result of falling into the canal or getting tossed into it. Boats — though cannallers didn't like to admit it — sometimes leaked so badly they sank. After the Erie was enlarged and deepened, a boat loaded with rock salt sprung a leak just east of Schenectady near Niskayuna. The captain was not sure he could beach the barge before it sank, so he grabbed a fire ax and began to hack away at the roof of the stable which housed two mules. As least they could swim off if the boat sank.

Presently an elderly woman appeared from below decks, and she began pleading with the captain to look after the cargo she was taking to New York City.

Some locktenders on shore spied the woman and shouted to the captain. "Never mind those mules," they hollered, "get that old lady off the boat before it goes down!"

The boater kept hacking away. "These mules cost money," he shouted back. "I can get an old lady any place!"

Along the Erie Canal in Schenectady.

111

Chapter 38

Justice Along the Erie

Sliding Down the Erie

During they heyday of the Ee-rye-ee, people of all sorts rode the canal boats. One time, a doxie boarded a boat for the trip from Buffalo to Troy. She must have behaved herself rather badly and certainly imbibed too much. When she arrived at the canal's eastern end, she was taken off the canal boat very much drunk and hauled before a town judge.

The judge asked her where she came from.

"I slid down from Buffalo on a plank," she told him.

"Well," said the judge, "to Albany County Jail for you for 180 days so you can pick the slivers out of your behind!"

The Jumper

Could anyone jump across the Erie? Samuel Hopkins Adams said that the good Squire Adams, his grandfather who worked on the canal, claimed no man ever spanned that forty foot breadth, but Sidecut folks felt differently. They knew one fellow around there who was aptly called "Jumper." He could run and jump like no other man on the canal. But Jumper was also light-fingered. When the sheriff and three deputies got on his trail and cornered him near the side of the lock, Jumper proved worthy of his name. He took one look at the law, leaped across the lock, and escaped justice for another day.

The Driver Boys' Winter Home

Two boys about sixteen years old walked into a canal town police court early in December 1870 and asked to be sent to the penitentiary until the opening of navigation in the spring. Incidents of this sort occurred rather commonly. They explained that they had been driving on the canal since May but had been cheated out of their wages and had no place to go.

When they both pleaded guilty to vagrancy, they were sent to jail for six months.

The Parrot That Talked Too Much

The wife of a tippling judge nagged him over his habit so much that the family parrot learned to say, "The judge is drunk again." One night when the judge arrived home much in the cups, the parrot started in with "The judge is drunk again. . ." That did it. His Honor pronounced sentence, and the talkative bird lost its life thereby.

'Nuff Said

Some old boater must have been having trouble with his family, and he was brought before the judge.

The judge started off by asking him if he knew the meaning of an oath. "Why, yessir," the man answered, "I worked on the canal for might' nigh forty years!"

Chapter 39

Skunk Tale

An old canaller used to run an "immigrant boat," bringing immigrant people up the Erie Canal.

Once he was coming to Syracuse with a boatload who had been living on macaroni so long, he said, they were crazy for fresh meat, so every time they'd see a woodchuck, somebody would jump ashore and take after it. The other side of Utica the steersman sees a big skunk over in a field, and he yelled, "Look, boys — a black and white woodchuck!" Well, about fifteen of these fellows jumped ashore and surrounded that skunk and started to throw stones at it.

Now, you know how a skunk acts when people start to heave stones at it, and this brute just sprayed those immigrant fellows with perfume. But were they discouraged? Not a bit. They killed the skunk and dragged it back to the boat. The steersman was pretty scared now because he thought maybe they'd take after him for putting them onto that skunk. But they just seemed to relax and they made stew out of that poor skunk, and ate it. They told the steersman it was one of the best flavored woodchucks they ever ate. But the boat was so smelly that the mules wouldn't come aboard, and the driver had to use the one team all the rest of the trip.

Chapter 40

Handsome
George Huntington

Rome's first canal commissioner, George Huntington, was also the first merchant in the city. He was a man of great character, and his personal appearance was considered to be very fine, an observation borne out by the fact that the Oneida Indians gave him a name ("A-i-o") which in their language meant "handsome."

Huntington had the distinction of taking the first canal toll on the Erie. It was paid by a Captain Westcott for, of all things, the passage of a raft of lumber.

Huntington indirectly helped Benjamin Wright's career on the Erie. At the time Englishman William Weston's Western Inland Lock Navigation Company was involved in constructing improvements at Little Falls and Wood Creek, Huntington borrowed the company's levelling instrument, took it to Wright and asked him to do a map and profile of Wood Creek. Benjamin Wright made the survey, prepared the map and profile to the complete satsifaction of the directors. This effort had a lot to do with their choice of Benjamin Wright as a chief engineer on the later Erie Canal project.

Chapter 41

Father of
American Civil Engineering

If New York State's Grand Canal was the first American school of civil engineering, Benjamin Wright was its dean. The early Erie engineers were self-made men and largely self-taught. There was no profession of engineering in the United States before them. Their influence is incalculable, for when their tasks on the Erie were done they went on to other civil engineering assignments, not only in New York State but throughout the East and the Midwest.

Benjamin Wright's career was perhaps the most varied among his contemporaries, and included roads, bridges, canals, and railroads. His assistants formed the nucleus of the American civil engineering profession in the first half of the nineteenth century, amounting to a virtual "school" of civil engineering in America.

He was born in Wethersfield, Connecticut, where he learned surveying from an uncle in nearby Plymouth. His family moved to Fort Stanwix (Rome), New York, when he was nineteen; and there he worked as farmer and land surveyor. Early versed in mathematics and surveying studies, young Wright soon became known among the settlers by making surveys and subdividing the extensive tracts of land surrounding Fort Stanwix. He laid out into farms, for instance, some 500,000 acres in Oneida and

Oswego counties. He was engaged by the British engineer, William Weston, when the Western Inland Lock and Navigation Company began its canal connection with the Mohawk River, a project which was, in fact, a precursor of the Erie. By the time the surveys for the statewide Erie Canal project had been made, Benjamin Wright was well established both as surveyor and a judge. He was selected to survey the eastern half of the canal route and, when canal construction began in 1817, Wright was named the engineer in charge of the Middle Section, where ground was broken at Rome on July 4, 1817.

The extent of Benjamin Wright's impact on the Canal Era in the United States can only be surmised, but some idea of his influence can be gleaned from the extensive list of projects in which he was engaged either as Chief Engineer or as principal consultant between 1824 and 1838: the Erie Canal (New York), Farmington Canal (Connecticut), Blackstone Canal (Rhode Island), Chesapeake and Delaware Canal (Delaware), Delaware and Hudson Canal (New York and Pennsylvania), Chesapeake and Ohio Canal (Maryland), Welland Canal (U.S. and Canada), James River and Kanawha Canal (Virginia), and Chicago-Illinois River Canal (Illinois). With his son, Benjamin Hall Wright, he was largely responsible for the first railroad in Cuba, built in 1834-1835, and he worked on various railroads in New York and other states.

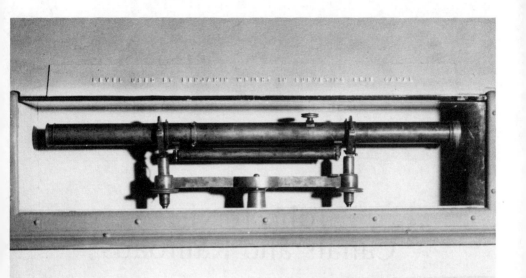

Surveyor's level used by Benjamin Wright in his canal surveys.

Stanwix Museum, Rome; Photo by D. Tranquille, Utica

NATIONAL HISTORIC
CIVIL ENGINEERING LANDMARK

AMERICAN
SOCIETY OF
CIVIL
ENGINEERS
FOUNDED
1852

THE ERIE CANAL

BEGUN AT ROME, NEW YORK
JULY 4, 1817   COMPLETED 1825

BENJAMIN WRIGHT (1770-1842) CHIEF ENGINEER

ASCE 1967

Chapter 42

John Jervis:
Canals and Railroads

A man's real place in history is often slow in being defined, but the artist who conceived and painted the mural in the lobby of the Manhattan Hotel in New York City showed an appreciation of great labors well performed when he selected John B. Jervis as one of the subjects of a life-size group consisting of Benjamin Franklin, with his kite and key; Samuel F.B. Morse, with his telegraph set; Robert Fulton with his steamboat; and John Jervis on bended knee presenting High Bridge Aqueduct to Father Knickerbocker.

Born in Huntington, New York, in 1795, young Jervis spent his teenage years assisting his father with farm work. At the age of twenty-two he hired on as axman on the Erie Canal project at Rome, and the record of his achievements after that shows he had energy, perseverance, and an unlimited capacity for hard work. In 1819 Jervis was resident engineer over a seventeen-mile section of the Erie, and in 1823 he became superintendent of canal construction for a fifty-mile section. In 1825 he resigned this position to plan the route for another New York waterway, the D & H Canal, and to superintend its construction until 1829. The next year he became Chief Engineer of the Mohawk & Hudson Railway and, later, of the Schenectady & Saratoga Railroad.

John B. Jervis and Mrs. Jervis seated on the front porch of their home in Rome, New York, circa 1880.

In 1833 the state's Canal Commissioners again engaged Jervis, this time as Chief Engineer for the Chenango Canal, one of the Erie's tributaries.

The first locomotive made for use in America was built according to Jervis's specifications, and his invention of the bogie truck in 1831 gave railroading an essential part of the equipment of practically all high-speed trains used in modern America. Later, he worked on the original Croton water supply system to New York City, including the famed High Bridge aqueduct. Jervis also supervised railroad building in Michigan, Indiana, and Illinois. In the twentieth century, the Delaware and Hudson Railroad named its finest locomotive after him.

Port Jervis, New York, also was named for him; but he preferred Rome, and that is where he settled down. He remained active, preferring, he said to "wear out rather than rust out," by running the Rome Merchant Iron Mill, writing two books, *Railroad Property* and *Labor and Capital*. In 1878 Hamilton College conferred on Jervis an honorary LL.D. degree. When he died in 1885 he left $50,000 to the city of Rome, including his residence, for a public library. Today, Jervis Public Library is one of the most popular and useful public institutions in the city.

Chapter 43

Did You Say You Drove
Under the Erie Canal?

"Nothing in all of motoring" said newspaperman Bill Ramale of Buffalo, "is quite like passing through the tunnel on Culvert Road in Orleans County." This stone subway at the foot of a slope, small and arched, makes it seem to the speeding motorist that he's going through the eye of a needle. The 7-foot, 6-inch clearance isn't what provides the special feeling for the driver. What does that is the fact that the 200-foot tunnel goes under the Erie Canal.

As early as 1824 Horatio Gates Spafford pointed out in his *Pocket Guide* that the town of Ridgeway had the only arch roadway under the Erie Canal. A new one was built for the enlarged canal, and the tunnel was retained for the later Barge Canal. All the crossings on today's canal system are fixed or lift bridges, except the underpass east of Medina, off Route 31 on Culvert Road. That tunnel is listed by the New York State Department of Public Works as Culvert 96.

In 1850 plans were drawn for another canal culvert at Holley, but the idea was dropped. The one near Medina stayed, however. When the Erie Canal was enlarged in 1854, engineers tore down a viaduct that had crossed Clinton's Ditch and installed the present tunnel to provide passage for farm wagons and pedestrians.

Well-qualified masons were assigned the project, cutting and fitting an archway of stone underneath the banks of the canal. When finished, the structure had a width at the bottom of fifteen feet and the peak of the curved ceiling measured thirteen feet from the ground. About fifty-five years later, another generation of engineers added sixty-four more feet to the length of the subway.

Culvert Road became a lightly travelled roadway through orchards and dairy country. On the canal bank — the Erie Barge Canal now — above the tunnel, rambling wooden fences separated pasture lands. Unless they glimpsed the hull of a passing boat, many motorists were unaware that the tunnel passed beneath a waterway, and even fewer knew that it goes back historically to the middle of the nineteenth century when the Old Erie was enlarged and even to the days before the Erie Canal was completed.

Chapter 44

The Worthington Steam Boat

While canal boats and mules (or horses) seem to go hand in hand in the lore of the Canal Era, other forms of boat power were being discussed even before the Erie project was completed. "The subject of propelling boats by steam on the Grand Canal," wrote a reporter in the *Onondaga Gazette* of October 1, 1823, "has long attracted the attention of speculative men," and he thought that there was "every probable reason to suppose some of their theories will be reduced to practice." In confirmation, he said, "we have the satisfaction of examining a few days past, a Steam Boat built in Pompey which passed this place, and bids fair to answer the purpose intended. Should it succeed, there can be little doubt of its being entitled to a preference, in point of economy, to the present mode of towing by means of horses."

This newspaper account is probably the earliest report of a steam canal boat on the Erie. The date is eight days before the eastern division of the canal was opened to the Hudson River and two years before the western division was completed and Governor Clinton set out from Buffalo on the first through boat to Albany.

William Avery of Buellville in Pompey built the boat, and floated it first on the Limestone Creek mill pond near his home.

He tested it further on Lake Owahgena at Cazenovia and finally put it on the canal. An historic marker on the road in Buellville commemorates the first launching of this early steam boat. William Avery was the uncle of John E. Sweet, inventor of the Straight Line engine and a founder and early president of the American Society of Mechanical Engineers.

In May 1829 a newspaper report from Utica described the efforts of two "ingenious mechanics of the village," Messrs. Rogers and Garrat by name, who were said to have invented a method of propelling boats on the canal by steam. Their invention, the account said, "promises to obviate the principal difficulties that have hitherto prevented the application of this power for that purpose." The Rogers-Garrat improvement consisted chiefly in causing the paddle to move horizontally through the water instead of being attached to a wheel. A model was reportedly on display in their factory, as they planned to build a boat based upon their design.

But it wasn't until the 1860's that steam was beginning to replace the horse as the main source of propulsion of Erie Canal boats. "A propeller went through here yesterday morning with five boatloads of coal, thus doing the work of ten horses," said a Schenectady journalist in 1862, noting that two more passed during the day. "In a very few years," the reporter added prophetically, "steam will supercede horsepower." A few years earlier, the *Asa P. Farr* raced the *Levi Willard* from Troy to Buffalo for a $500 prize. The *Asa P.* won by eight hours. It took four days and eight hours to cover the distance. Its speed was about three miles per hour.

Progress-minded New Yorkers tried many an idea to try to retire the horses and mules. A man named Dean, who owned a drydock in Utica, invented a steamboat with a wheel that was to run on a rail along the canal. He built the boat, but it didn't work, and everybody called it "Dean's Folly" after that. In later barge-boat days, it was said that the General Electric Company developed and tried "electric mules." They didn't catch on, either. Apparently, progress wasn't always GE's most reliable product.

Steam power, actually, should have been on the canal long before it was. The Worthington Corporation in Buffalo (originally in Brooklyn) dates from the first pump its founder, Henry

R. Worthington, installed on his own canal boat in 1840. It worked, but it worked too well. The State of New York gave Worthington a medal but told him to stop trying to create steam canal boats.

It seems that the state, in its enthusiasm to further progress, invited engineers and inventors to design a steam boat for use on the Erie Canal. The Worthington design was a boat equipped with two paddle wheels, at either side of the forward portion of the hull. The blades were set at an angle, so that instead of throwing the wake against the easily eroded walls of the canal, they directed it toward the stern of the boat.

The principal challenge in those days was to produce a pump for the boiler that could operate when the boat was not in motion. The practice was to feed boilers by pumps connected directly with the main engine shaft; thus, unless the main engine was in motion, the pump was idle. Whenever a boat passed through lockage, the engine was stopped and the water level in the boiler dropped. The only way to raise the level again was to pump the water in by hand, taking time and hard labor. After studying the problem, Worthington tossed precedent aside and designed a pump, powered by the steam in the boiler, that acted independently to maintain boiler water level. He put the pump cylinders in a straight line and eliminated the customary flywheel and beam mechanism. He had built, in 1840, the first direct-acting steam pump in history, and it worked fine. But that was the catch, as it turned out.

Although Worthington's steam canal boat operated on the canal several seasons, it was not looked on in favor by the boaters, farmers, innkeepers and others who depended upon the canal for a livelihood. There was a storm of protests over the steam canal boat. The Legislature appointed a committee to investigate. They studied the new boat and its operation, complimented the young designer, voted him a medal to commemorate his achievement, and then directed him to give up any futher activities concerning steam canal boating.

Removed from the Erie boat, Worthington's first pump operated efficiently for more than thirty years. Later on, Worthington showed it off at his plant and loaned it out for display. At a machinery exhibition in Pittsburgh the original was badly damaged by fire. The Smithsonian Institution in Washington, however, has a model of Worthington's first steam pump in the National Museum of American History, along with a second pump and many early Worthington Corporation drawings. In 1899, Worthington absorbed a Buffalo firm, the Snow Steam Pump works, henceforth known as Worthington's Snow or the Buffalo Works.

Worthington went on to become an important and successful supplier of Navy equipment. In 1850, the *USS Susquehanna* was the first Navy ship to have Worthington equipment, as did the two Civil War ironclads, the *Merrimac* and the *Monitor*. The Worthington Corporation plant built hundreds of compressors for the Navy during World War II and afterwards continued to supply equipment for all classes of Navy vessels, including Polaris submarines. But Henry R. Worthington got his start with a dream of building a steam powered fleet for the Erie Canal, capable of going right through from Buffalo to Albany and down the Hudson to New York City in the 1840's.

Full-size replica of Henry Worthington's first steam pump in the National Museum of American History.

Chapter 45

The *William Newman*
Sets a Record

When you hear of steam power putting mule power out of business on the Erie, you naturally think of the railroads which eventually did win the larger part of the transportation battle as the nineteenth century wore on. Or the steam boats. One of the best of these was the *William Newman* of Buffalo, which was designed and built by a practical canal man in the winter and spring of 1872. It was made of the best white oak, second growth chestnut and pine, well fastened with iron and preserved with salt, and modeled after the best Erie Canal boats then in use. The *William Newman* was ninety-eight feet overall, with a ninety-two foot keel and 17.5-foot beam. She was light, too. Including machinery and water in the boiler, she weighed about seventy-five tons and had a carrying capacity of 220 tons.

The cost of the hull and all onboard machinery was $7000. The boat's machinery consisted of a simple upright noncondensing engine, with a small "Donkey" engine and pump for feeding the boiler and for fire protection. The boiler and engine occupied no more space than was allotted on the horse boats to a stable. The four-bladed, five-foot-diameter screw pushed the *William Newman* through the water at an average speed of four miles per hour at seven-feet depth and six miles per hour in deeper wide water. Its coal consumption was a hundred pounds an hour or thirty-four pounds of fuel per mile of canal.

On November 5, 1873, the *William Newman* arrived in Buffalo from Troy after running a distance of 345 miles through seventy-two locks in the extraordinary time of four days and twenty-two hours. Allowing for stops, that translates to three days and ten hours of running time with a 121-ton cargo.

Steam-powered canal boat, William Newman, *in Buffalo, 1873*

Chapter 46

Captain Leonard's
John F. Dean

The 240-ton *John F. Dean*, captained by Elisher Leonard, was the first canal boat to attempt to go from New York to Buffalo under her own gasoline power. For fourteen years the *Dean* had been just another three-mule-power canal boat in a fleet of fifty owned by William Warwick, a canal boat insurance man in Buffalo. Then her owner had an automobile engine installed on the afterdeck. The engine, according to Captain Leonard, could turn the thirty-inch screw some 650 times a minute without half trying.

"Mules can cover only about ten miles during the whole forepart watch of six hours," said Captain Leonard in a newspaper interview the day before the first gasoline run. "Now, believe me or not," he said, his boat was going to "smash along" at a right good clip.

"Onless," commented Jim Snee, of the boat's crew, "them farmer fellers upstate with tin stars on their coats git out speed reg'lations." Snee was apprehensive of country constables. "They're sore on automobiles," he explained, referring to western New York, "an' you c'n see yourself that this here craft ain't no different now from a racin' red devil, 'cept that she's painted white an' has 'em skinned for size."

Snee and Leonard also felt that their boat had a considerable advantage over the new-fangled automobiles they called the "chug-chug carts."

"What dust they is on the water is mud," they said, "and can't git into a feller's eyes." They wouldn't need any big green goggles like the automobilists, "onless," Snee added, thoughtfully, "the wind gits too strong when we get hittin' up a four-mile clip."

Even with mechanical engines, boaters were true to the tradition that sailing Erie water took second place to nothing else.

This Captain Leonard of the *John F. Dean*, like all boatmen, idolized Grover Cleveland, because of what was felt to be Cleveland's influence in abolishing the canal tolls. Cleveland's election, boaters say, helped to defeat the tax. During his campaign for Governor in 1882, Leonard's boat floated a banner with "CLEVELAND AND A FREE CANAL." It was painted on in red letters, and the *New York Sun* said it was the only political banner on the Erie.

Chapter 47

Cleveland's Favorite Tavern

Grover Cleveland grew up in canal territory, and in some ways the Erie fashioned his political career. At the very least the canal was a backdrop to much of it.

At mid-century, his Presbyterian minister father moved the family from Fayetteville, just east of Syracuse, New York, to Clinton, possibly in the hope that there his sons might attend Hamilton College, then as now a small college with a big reputation. Cleveland, his wife and five children were admitted to membership in the Stone Church of Clinton in May 1851. His son Grover was highly active in the church for several years and went on to Buffalo in 1855 to study law, served as mayor of that city, and in 1884 was elected President of the United States.

Both before and after he became Mayor of Buffalo, Grover Cleveland generally shied away from canal saloons. He also preferred German brews to hard liquor.

One of the future President's favorite spots, according to newspaperman George Condon, was a Buffalo tavern known as "The Shades." Owned and operated by a man named Smith, The Shades was a no-nonsense drinkng establishment. It had no bar and no bartender. It offered standing room only, a saloon without tables, chairs, or booths. Its walls were lined with barrels and kegs containing beers, whiskeys, wines and brandies. In the center of the tavern were two tables, with clean glasses on one and loose money on the other.

The system was simple. A customer took a glass from the first table, filled it from the barrel or keg of his choice, then dropped off the price of the drink on the money table. He made his own change, if necessary, from the loose coins and paper money.

Smith believed in the innate honesty of man, and he had remarkable trust in his saloon customers. For Cleveland, as Condon suggests, The Shades perhaps represented the kind of integrity he himself so much admired.

Late nineteenth century view of Black Rock, at the Buffalo end of the canal, showing guard locks south of Austin Street.

Buffalo & Erie County Historical Society

Chapter 48

Menlo Park on the Erie

You might say that the Westinghouse Company really got its start along the Erie Canal.

George Westinghouse, Jr., the inventor and founder of the company, was born in 1846 in the nearby village of Central Bridge, where his father ran a small machinery shop. Eight years later the shop was moved to Schenectady, next to the Erie Canal on River Road — the same site later occupied by another historic enterprise, Radio Station WGY.

Obviously a man with a keen mind, George apparently hid his abilities well, and he had a reputation for appearing more lazy than industrious. He puttered around his father's machinery shop, took courses at Schenectady's Union College and, over in Troy, at Rensselaer Polytechnic Institute, all the while playing around inventing things. His college professors thought him "dull and backward" as a student, and said he would never amount to much.

So much for academic opinion. His laziness did, however, get him thrown out of the family business, so he went across town to the American Locomotive Works, also a pioneer Schenectady enterprise, where he perfected the air brake that would make him famous and "Westinghouse Co." a household word. He patented the brake in 1869 and set up his own business in Pittsburgh.

Electricity soon followed, with an AC/DC battle, for it wasn't long before he began experiments with alternating current to become a rival of Edison Electric Works, located back in Schenectady. Founded in 1866, the Edison Works preferred direct current, until it became General Electric Company in 1891. In the meantime, George's father's business, now a farm equipment company, kept the rest of the Westinghouses and the name right under GE's nose where the canal came through Schenectady.

The Westinghouse Company along the Erie Canal in Schenectady, south of the Washington Avenue bridge, with General Electric buildings in the background.

John P. Papp

Chapter 49

The Circus

Travelling circuses and theatre groups once brought glitter and glamour to country folk, and upstate New York was no exception. As an artery of commerce, the Erie Canal opened more towns and villages across New York State to the actors and actresses who "trod the boards" or the circus performers who delighted children of all ages with their grease-paint clowns, daredevil animal acts, and spectacular showmanship on the highwire or flying trapeze.

Author Samuel Hopkins Adams, for one of whose ancestors the canal hamlet of Adams Basin is named, memorialized the travelling theatre troupes in his novel *Banner by the Wayside*, which shows how closely such performances as those of the Thaila "T" Troupe were tied to Erie water. Walter D. Edmonds did a similar thing for the circus in his novel *Chad Hanna*. Chad was an Erie lad from Canastota, who put his lot in with that of Huguenine's Circus as it made its way through the central upstate area. Actor Henry Fonda had the role of Chad Hanna in the movie version. Fonda, who had already played the Erie boater Dan Harrow in *The Farmer Takes a Wife*, was on the way to making a trademark of his Yorker twang and manner.

Both of these two instances are fictional. The Sautelle Circus

137

Sig Sautelle's circus boats tied up at the Farmer's Market in Clinton Square, Syracuse.

Canal Society of New York State

was another matter.

Sig Sautelle was a showman, start to finish. He was born in Luzerne, New York, September 22, 1848, and went to school in that Adirondack village. During the Civil War he enlisted in the Union Army and was proud of the fact that he was regarded as the youngest voluntary enlistee. During his military stint, he met a ventriloquist who taught Sig his art, which gave him an additional bit of theatrical expertise in his later showman years.

Actually, he was not born Sig. His real name was George Saterlee, but he adopted the name of Signor Sautelle when he launched his first Punch and Judy show. His face, however, lacked the Latin look and, besides, no one ever pronounced the second syllable of "Signor" anyway, so he became simply Sig Sautelle.

His circus boat, with its big letters painted on the side saying "SIG SAUTELLE'S BIG SHOWS," was the pride of the Erie Canal and the envy of many a competitor. Sautelle's name meant clean entertainment at a modest price, and Sig Sautelle became one of the most highly respected showmen in the New York canal region. Sautelle used Homer, New York, as his headquarters during all this time. He also purchased a hotel there which he called the David Harum House, since Homer was known as the home of the person upon whom Edward Noyes Westcott based his famous title character in his *David Harum* novel, published in 1899. Sautelle rather startled people around Homer with his three octagon-shaped buildings, which he liked because they resembled a circus tent as much as possible. One building was an animal barn, one the training barn, and one was his own residence.

In 1904, Sautelle let James McCaddon of the Barnum Show, who was looking for a show to take to France, use his for $120,000. After that, he formed a partnership with Welsh Brothers, of Lancaster, Pennsylvania, but when that didn't last he returned to Homer. By 1914, Mrs. Sautelle had died and Sig sold out the Sautelle show and tried to retire from show business. He couldn't, though. Nearing seventy, he formed the Sig Sautelle & Oscar Lawanda Mammoth Motor Truck Circus and, finally, the Humpty Dumpty Circus, a Punch and Judy show. He played schools and clubs with it, ending his career as he began it.

In his heyday, Sig Sautelle always let the calendar decide his

139

opening. He was not a superstitious man, and it was known that he always would open his show on a Friday if he could, as near as possible to the 13th of the month. He was jubilant when the 13th fell on a Friday.

Hollywood treatment of circus life on the Erie Canal in the 1830's.

Chapter 50

Riding Fog

The last big fog in the Irondequoit Valley, near Rochester, New York, appears to have been in 1873. It was a humdinger, they say.

As a canal boat with a new driverboy was passing through Rochester and over the Genesee River aqueduct, the fog began to roll in. It blanketed the towpath and spread for miles around. The boy was leading the mules, and after he'd passed Bushnell Basin, he missed the towpath altogether and struck off north.

The steersman on that canal boat was too full of applejack to notice what was happening. At daybreak, as the fog began to lift, the mules were just starting to wade into Lake Ontario water. They had "rode fog" and dragged that canal boat nearly twenty miles over dry land!

New York Waterways

142

Chapter 51

Cap'n Jason

Some oldtime canal boat captains were real eccentrics. Take the case of Cap'n Jason, who always wore a uniform like a Rear Admiral. Captain Hanks of the *Tilly Schlitz* liked to tell how Cap'n Jason just loved to see Erie boats race.

He'd get so het up during a race, said Hanks, what with leaning out over the bow and shouting, that he'd near fall overboard every time from excitement! One day he did. On the stretch to Albany, Cap'n Jason hollered over to Hanks, "If you beat that Jackson boat t' th' dock, I'll git you a new suit of clothes in Albany." Then he leaned out too far, and over he went into the canal. (Hanks got the suit, incidentally. Seems he liked to race, too.)

Captain Hanks told of another time he was steering between the Lockport locks about dusk.

"Hard a-port!" yells Cap'n Jason, all of a sudden from the bow of his boat. "I thought he meant starb'd," related Captain Hanks later in an interview, "but I throwed 'er to port as ordered, an' we skinned twenty feet of new planking off on the rocks!"

"Damn it!" yells Cap'n Jason. "Don't you know I mean 'starb'd' when I say 'port'?"

"They don't grow men like Cap'n Jason now," Captain Hanks observed wryly.

"Along the Erie Canal" by Arthur B. Davies, 1890.

Phillips Collection, Washington, D.C.

Great Seal of the State of New York

Index

147

148

91, 94;
and Mark Twain, 87-88;
food and meals on, 90-92;
canal boat cooks, 94-95;
whales on, 98, 99;
saloons and taverns, 107-108, 133;
judges and justices on, 112-114;
engineers, 116, 117-118, 120, 121,
126-128;
steam powered boats on, 125-128,
129-130, 131-132;
canal boat racing on, 126, 143-144;
and Grover Cleveland, 132;
and George Westinghouse, Jr., 135-
136;
and Sautelle's circus, 137-139;
in movies, 137, 140
See also Folklore
Erie Canal Village (Rome, N.Y.) 27, 28

Farmer Takes a Wife, The, 137
Fayetteville, 27
Fitch, Asa:
his *Diary* of the Rensselaer School
expedition, 53-56, 104
Folklore:
in upstate New York, xi;
and the Erie Canal, xi-xii, 23;
St. Nicholas and the Erie, 29-30;
Rexford tavern tale, 45;
ridding the towpath of snakes, 61-62;
boxing, 57-58;
fighting canallers, 59-60;
boater's tale, 63-65;
drunken fish, 64;
canal mosquitoes, 70;
trained mules, 71;
fish story, 72-73;
the giant frog of Empeyville, 74-75;
the strongest boater, 77-78;
ballads and songs, 79-83, 85-86, 91,
94, 95;
food lore, 90-92;
canal cooks, 94-95;
Catskill Johnny Darling, 96-97;
Edmonds's whale story, 98-100;
canal corn lot, 102;
clover seed tale, 102;
giant squash, 105-106;
saloons and taverns, 107-108, 133-
134;
Schenectady stories, 109-110;
canal justice, 112-114;
immigrants-woodchuck tale, 115;
canal boat races, 126, 143-144;

Sautelle's canal circus, 137-140;
the big fog, 141
Fonda, Henry, 137, 140
Fort Orange. *See* Albany
Fort Plain, 91
Fort Stanwix, 23, 55, 117
See also Rome
Frankfort, 26, 66
Gasport, 44, 56, 103, 104
Geddes, James:
on origin of the Erie Canal, 22;
biography and career of, 50-51
General Electric Company, 126, 136
Genesee Level. *See* Long Level
Gerstaecker, Frederick:
comments on canal breakfast, 90
Governor Clinton (Lafayette's packet
boat), 37, 38
Grandfather Stories, xii

Hamilton College, 54, 96, 122
Hancock, John, 26
Hart, Larry:
quoted, 109-110
Hawley, Jesse:
proponent of Erie Canal and his
"Hercules" articles, 21-22
Henry, Joseph, 54
"Hercules." *See* Hawley, Jesse
Herkimer, 47
Holmes, Oliver Wendell, 37
Howells, William Dean, 75
Huntington, George, 116

"Im Afloat" (song), 80

Jagendorf, Moritz:
quoted on John Darling, 96
James, Jesse, 58
Jervis, John B., 120-122
Jervis Public Library (Rome), 122

Kemble, Frances, 55

Lafayette, Marquis de:
on Staffordshire china, 34;
tours the Erie Canal, 35-39;
painting of, 36
Lambertville, Pa., 27
Lehigh Canal (Pa.), 27
"Life on the Canawl" (song), 81
Little Falls, 25, 34, 55, 116
Lock Berlin, 27
Lockport, 31-32, 67

149